D1029070

BLOOD IN THE BADLANDS

A Warhammer Campaign

Shane S.

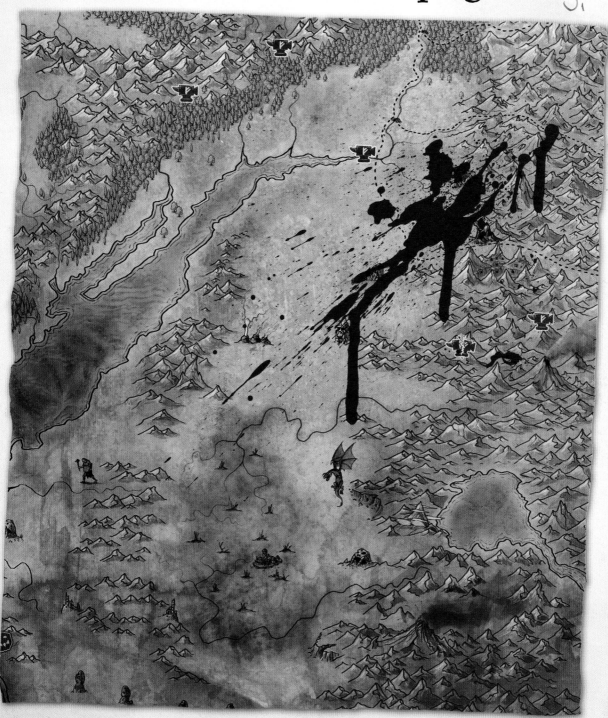

CONTENTS

Written and produced by Studio White Dwarf: Simon Grant, Andy Hall, Tom Hutchings, Matthew Hutson, Andrew Kenrick, Jim Shardlow & Kris Shield.
With Additional Contributions by: Kevin Chin, Pete Foley, Jervis Johnson, Chris Peach & Markus Trenkner.
Art: John Blanche, Alex Boyd, Kevin Chin, Paul Dainton, Dave Gallagher, Neil Hodgson, Nuala Kinrade & John Michelbach. **'Eavy Metal:** Neil Green, David Heathfield, Mark Holmes, Matt Kennedy, Kornel Kozak, Joe Tomaszewski & Anja Wettergren. **Mighty Empires Kit Design:** Mark Jones. **Miniatures Design:** Mike Anderson, Giorgio Bassani, Trish Carden, Ed Cottrell, Juan Diaz, Martin Footitt, Michael Fores, Colin Grayson, Jes Goodwin, Mark Harrison, Alex Hedström, Nick Ho, Matt Holland, Neil Langdown, Darren Latham, Aly Morrison, Brian Nelson, Gavin Newton, Oliver Norman, Seb Perbet, Alan Perry, Michael Perry, Dale Stringer, Dave Thomas & Tom Walton.
Production & Reprographics: Simon Burton, Chris Eggar, Marc Elliott, Zaff Haydn-Davies, Kris Jaggers, Melissa Roberts, Rachel Ryan & James Shardlow.

Copyright © Games Workshop Limited 2011. All Rights Reserved. Games Workshop, the Games Workshop logo, 'Eavy Metal, Citadel and the Citadel device are either ®, TM and/or © Games Workshop Ltd 2000-2011, variably registered in the UK and other countries around the world. All Rights Reserved.

Games Workshop, the Games Workshop logo, GW, Citadel, the Citadel device, Citadel Finecast, Warhammer, Warhammer logo, Warhammer Armies, The Game of Fantasy Battles, the twin-tailed comet device, Warhammer 40,000, the Warhammer 40,000 logo, 40K, 40,000, the double-headed eagle/Aquila design, White Dwarf and all associated marks, logos, names, places, characters, creatures, races and race insignia, illustrations and images from the Warhammer world and Warhammer 40,000 universe are either R, TM and/or C Games Workshop Ltd 2000-2011 variably registered around the world. All Rights Reserved.

UK	**Northern Europe**	**North America**	**Australia**
Games Workshop Ltd.,	Games Workshop Ltd,	Games Workshop Inc,	Games Workshop,
Willow Rd, Lenton,	Willow Rd, Lenton,	6211 East Holmes Road,	23 Liverpool Street,
Nottingham,	Nottingham,	Memphis,	Ingleburn,
NG7 2WS	NG7 2WS, UK	Tennessee 38141	NSW 2565

www.games-workshop.com

INTRODUCTION

Over the course of the past twelve months, some of the Studio's most dedicated hobbyists have been busy, fighting it out for domination of the Badlands. In this book we tell the tale of their bloody campaign.

When I was younger and first getting into the hobby (some twenty years ago now), I avidly read every issue of White Dwarf, poring over every beautifully painted miniature, reading every scrap of background and rule, and loving every last word of the battle reports. But there was one type of article that I was sure to read first, yet return to over and over again, and that was campaign articles.

To this day, I still remember the very first Studio Mighty Empires campaign, wherein Jervis' Orc Warboss was captured by High Elves and forced to wear silk pyjamas (oh the ignominy!); I remember the Piscina IV campaign, with the sweeping advance by Andy Chambers' army of Dark Angels halted by the barbaric Orks, and Nazdreg's kunnin' tellyporta attack; and I can vividly recall every tank trap and booby-trapped street in the bloody cityfights of the Vogen V campaign. These campaigns just seemed like so much fun, spawning tales of great heroism and famous last stands. Just typing these words brings back fond memories and makes me want to delve into the White Dwarf archive to find those issues to relive again…

So you can probably imagine the excitement I had after joining the White Dwarf team, when I was first asked to play in a Studio campaign. And do you know what? It didn't disappoint, and the twists and turns of the Rok of Ages, the Return to Armageddon or Jervis' unnamed Warhammer campaign were every bit as fun as the campaigns I'd read about all those years ago.

And that's what this book is – it's a tale of our latest Studio campaign, recording our bloody battles, treacherous acts and heroic deeds. When we set out to play our latest campaign, we gathered as a group and came up with a list of all the things we wanted to see in a campaign – crusading armies, crazy Storm of Magic games, Warhammer battles with a sense of place and the occasional climactic game that brought everyone together. And what you see here is the result, a book all about our campaign.

First and foremost, this book is meant to entertain you with stories of our own exploits, but hopefully it will also inspire you to fight your own campaigns – or at least aspire to one day. To that end we've included the rules that we used, so you can play your own Blood in the Badlands campaign. We've also crammed in as many of the scenarios, spells, magic items and rules for sieges and underground battles as we could so that you can try them out in your own games.

And hopefully in years to come you'll look back on the Blood in the Badlands campaign fondly too and remember the tales of Ifrit Skybound's treachery, King Nekhenaten's tendency to get captured, Stiegfried Schweinsteiger's incessant poetry or the moment when Faelar Bladestorm was turned into a Clanrat.

Remember – victory is fleeting, but legendary deeds live on forever.

Andrew Kenrick

A YEAR IN THE BADLANDS

"The omens are true, my lord, the oracles correct; after a thousand years, Fozzrik's Flying Fastness has returned to the Old World. Wrought by magical artifice long lost to scholars of the arcane and coveted by emperors and kings the world over, the Flying Fastness is a sight to behold. A castle as large as any in your lands and crowned by eight spires swirling with all the Winds of Magic, the Flying Fastness would be a marvel even if it was grounded. But it is the feature that gives it its name: the peculiar magical effect wrought by Fozzrik himself that makes it so desirable – the blasted thing flies, soaring far above the land, unassailable by all.

Yet if the legends hold true, in a year's time the fortress will land for just one day, its gates opening and its magical wards abating long enough for a ready hero to lead his men within and seize control before the fastness takes to the skies once more. He who can claim such a treasure will dominate the skies above the world and rule the lands beneath its path. But mark my words – you will not be the only one to lay such a claim."

The legend of Fozzrik is swathed in mystery. He lived long before the establishment of the Colleges of Magic, yet the few surviving historical records agree that he was a powerful wielder of the arcane. How he came to be tutored in magic remains unknown.

A magus of ancient times who lived when the Empire was still young, all that is really known about the wizard is gleaned from the only grimoire Fozzrik is known to have authored. On the tome's dusty pages – which is now located deep within the vaults of the Grey College, where it is held as an arcane curiosity – Fozzrik wrote of his desire to create buildings that would move from place to place, cutting out the need for roads; where trade between towns would flourish when they contacted each other – in a quite literal sense – and whole cities could take to the air to traverse dense and dangerous forests or avoid rampaging armies. Even in those more unstable ancient times he was derided as a strange eccentric. Nevertheless Fozzrik's obsession with creating eldritch architecture continued unabated. The manipulation of stone and the imbuing of buildings with magical energy became his specialty.

What scholars of arcane history do agree on is that at the height of his power he retreated into the Badlands and there built a great fastness with Archimancy. The fortress was as imposing as it was beautiful, and impossible to conquer as a few bandit kings and marauding greenskins found out to lethal cost. But the motives for Fozzrik creating his castle had yet to be realised.

Fozzrik began to experiment, using his Archimancy to make buildings mobile, first by folding them in on themselves, to reduce their mass so they could be carried in a pouch or pocket. His real breakthrough was when he concocted a spell that made stone lighter than air, and so the floating towers of Fozzrik have been seen intermittently throughout the world ever since.

However, it was with his final Archimantic spell that he freed an entire fastness off the ground. It is said that the mage entered his castle and it took flight, never to land again… until now.

Legend states that Fozzrik's Flying Fastness has spent the last millennium soaring across the world, appearing only briefly at certain locales to gather mystical artefacts and powerful relics. The motives for doing so remain unclear, but many now suspect that the contents of the Flying Fastness are probably the greatest collection of eldritch antiquities to ever be assembled.

Whilst many have tried to plot the course of the Flying Fastness over the years, no doubt with larceny in mind, none have ever been successful. But that could be about to change. The Flying Fastness has returned to the Badlands, and it brings with it a great magical tempest. If the auguries are to be believed it is said that Fozzrik's spell is coming to an end. As the thousand-year conjuration dissipates it is creating a massive backlash in the Winds of Magic, generating violent magical storms in the castle's wake. If the seers are to be believed, the Flying Fastness must come to rest on the original ground it was built on; only then can the powerful spell be recast and the fortress take to the air once more.

This means that, for a short time at least, the Flying Fastness will be vulnerable and its treasures within reach. But where will it land? No records tell of where Fozzrik originally raised his enchanted castle, only that it was somewhere within the Badlands.

And so, with a year to go, the Flying Fastness is seen circling the skies, preparing to make landfall. Armies hastily gather, invading the Badlands and laying claim to vast areas, hoping that the Flying Fastness will come to rest in their domains so they can claim the castle itself. Only time will tell – four seasons to be precise – who will come to rule the Badlands and gain the ultimate prize.

Fozzrik's Flying Fastness – the ultimate prize for all the armies – as represented on our campaign map.

THE BADLANDS

The Badlands have ever been a dangerous place, riven by conflict as many greenskin tribes claim the region as their own. Under normal circumstances other races would shun the whole area, but the lure of the Flying Fastness has proven too strong.

The Badlands is the name given to the desolate landscape that stretches between the towering Worlds Edge Mountains in the east, the volcanic Dragonback Mountains in the west, the petty kingdoms of the Border Princes in the north and the foetid Marshes of Madness in the south. It is a land well named for it is notorious for the numerous greenskin tribes that prowl its wastes, not to mention the degenerate remnants of fallen civilisations and armies of bandits, criminals and worse. To venture into the Badlands is to take your life in your hands, for safe travel is impossible, even to those accompanied by a large army. Even without the inhospitable nature of its inhabitants, the Badlands are a harsh and unforgiving landscape, arid plains and wind-blasted moors. The land is littered with storm-tossed boulders and the evidence of dead civilisations; a traveller does not have to travel far before stumbling upon a ruin or a cairn… or an untimely and undoubtedly violent end.

A map of the Badlands

Making the Map

We made our map from two sets of Mighty Empires tiles, basing its layout on the map of the Badlands taken from Warhammer: Orcs & Goblins. We also used the Mighty Empires Expansions Tile Pack and the Campaign Markers set, along with a few extra components found in our collective bitz boxes.

The Orc fortress of Mount Bloodhorn

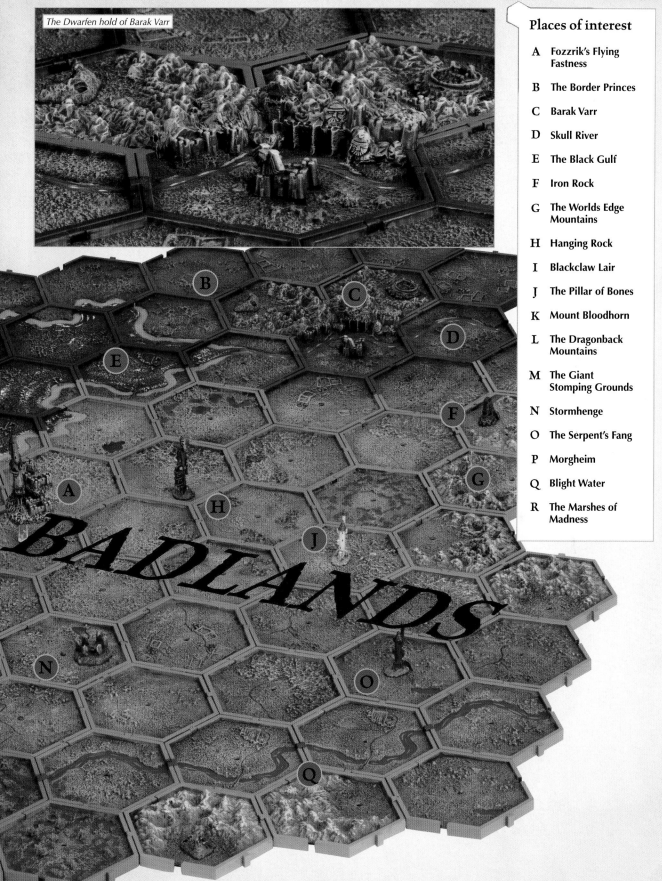

The Dwarfen hold of Barak Varr

Places of interest

A   Fozzrik's Flying
    Fastness

B   The Border Princes

C   Barak Varr

D   Skull River

E   The Black Gulf

F   Iron Rock

G   The Worlds Edge
    Mountains

H   Hanging Rock

I   Blackclaw Lair

J   The Pillar of Bones

K   Mount Bloodhorn

L   The Dragonback
    Mountains

M   The Giant
    Stomping Grounds

N   Stormhenge

O   The Serpent's Fang

P   Morgheim

Q   Blight Water

R   The Marshes of
    Madness

BADLANDS

A GUIDE TO THE BADLANDS

Although barren and blasted, the Badlands are not devoid of natural features and landmarks, from the impregnable fortress of Barak Varr in the north to the sinister and haunted remnants of the dead city of Morgheim.

Pirates of the Black Gulf

From the Bay of Wrecks to the very harbours of Barak Varr, the Pirates of the Black Gulf have been a thorn in the side of merchants and traders for years beyond remembering. Consisting of a motley fleet ranging from Sartosan galleons to the seafaring Orc hulk known as the Waaaghpig, the Pirates of the Black Gulf are arguably the principle reason that the formidable sea defences of Barak Varr are so vigorously maintained. It is the pirates' continued presence that requires regular patrols by the Ironclads of the Dwarf navy, and skirmishes are a frequent occurrence.

The Border Princes

Separated from the Empire by the Black Mountains, the Border Princes are a loose confederation of fiefdoms and robber barons. Those who are unhappy with the status quo in the Empire will often leave for a 'better life' in the Border Princes. But what they will find is a land even more dangerous than their previous home, where petty princelings war on each other, farmsteads are raided by marauding greenskins and pirates from Sartosa will come looking for plunder and slaves.

Barak Varr

Whilst the Badlands are devoid of any civilisation, there remains one bastion of Order located in the north. That is the ancient Dwarf Sea Fortress of Barak Varr. Wrought into the sides of the massive cliffs where the land meets the sea of the Black Gulf, Barak Varr is home to the Dwarfen fleet of invincible iron ships.

Great cavernous harbours that link directly to the sea protect the Dwarf fleet and those who visit the stronghold by sea.

This has led to Barak Varr becoming the most cosmopolitan of all the Dwarf holds. It is where traders from across the world will meet in relatively safety bringing in goods bound for further into the rest of the Dwarfen empire, or even northwards into the Border Princes and beyond.

Barak Varr has been assailed before but never taken, from above it is all-but impregnable, as the heart of the hold is located deep underground within the cliffs themselves. To try and take Barak Varr by sea means facing the Dwarf fleet of Ironclad paddle steamers, covered in swivel-cannon turrets as well as the formidable gun batteries studded into the cliff face of Barak Varr itself. None have even been successful; the bottom of the Black Gulf is littered with the vessels of those to have tried.

Dok Karaz

The gatehouse to Barak Varr, the fortress looms over the straits that lead into the Dwarf hold. It bristles with cannons and is topped with a mighty stone lighthouse that can be seen for leagues around.

The Black Gulf

The north-west coast of the Badlands borders the Black Gulf, a vicious sea that is notoriously difficult to navigate. Only the Dwarfs can trundle up and down the straits with constant regularity, as their ships' iron hulls and steam-driven paddles are somewhat immune to the ripping tides and deadly currents that swirl underneath the dark water. That's not to say the ships of other races cannot sail upon the Black Gulf, but they must be master seamen to do so, or else they will find their vessels quickly torn asunder.

Iron Rock

The Orc stronghold in the north of the Badlands is known as Iron Rock. It is a mountain formed of molten iron, vomited from the bowels of the earth during some ancient upheaval. The Dwarfs first discovered the mountain's rich seams and created a labyrinth of partially finished mineworks, but before they could extract the valuable resources held within, the Orcs arrived. Despite the Dwarfs' continued claim to the mountain, for over 800 years it has remained firmly in greenskin hands. The legendary Warboss, Gorbad Ironclaw, forever secured Iron Rock's dominance of the northern tribes by defeating Crusher Zorgoth and so uniting both Ironclaws and Broken Tooth tribes into a powerful tribal union that has subjugated the area ever since.

Hanging Rock

There are many dark places in the world, and the jutting stone shelf known as Hanging Rock is one such place. A battle was fought here, long ago. At the height of the battle, the hired mercenaries turned on their employers in a grand act of treachery. Their betrayal was their undoing, for to the dismay of the mercenaries, their employers won the day and swiftly enacted vengeance. Gallows were erected and the whole regiment hanged. As their blood seeped into the ground, the land around Hanging Rock was forever cursed.

Mount Bloodhorn (Ekrund)

The mightiest mountain in the Dragonbacks is known as Mount Bloodhorn, a greenskin stronghold swarming with Orcs that exerts its influence over the whole mountain chain and deep into the south of the Badlands. Before the coming of the Orcs, the mountain was mined by the Dwarfs from the settlement of Ekrund, nestled into the mountainside. The Dwarfs dug deep into the rock, creating a tunnel network that joined with naturally occurring caves, which the Orcs would later use to turn the mountain into a fortress. Deep in the mountain, within these cavernous chambers the residents of Mount Bloodhorn farm its greatest export, Cave Squigs. Squigs are bred here in their thousands and thus Night Goblins, whose Squig-herding expertise is unsurpassed, are also prevalent.

Orc & Goblin tribes of the Badlands

Since the infamous Battle of Blackfire Pass when Sigmar and his foundling Empire hurled back an enormous greenskin invasion, the Badlands have been infested with greenskins of all kinds. Unable to gain a permanent foothold in the lands of the Empire, Orc and Goblin tribes have made their lairs across the Border Princes, the Badlands and the vast mountain ranges that encircle those barren lands. The Dragonback Mountains in particular have long been a locus of greenskin activity, and the largest peak of them all, Mount Bloodhorn, has become something of a spiritual home to the tribes in the area. Yet this wretched fortress is far from the only greenskin lair, and warbands regularly roam from Iron Rock in the far north, Crooked Fang Fort in the east and Misty Mountain in the south.

The mystery of the Floating Village

The origins of the Floating Village are shrouded in mystery. The primitive huts and wooden longhouse that make up the village itself float twenty feet above the ground yet never seem to be affected by the fierce winds that sweep across the region. During the day the village is tethered to the ground, but at sunset the ropes are released and the village floats back into the sky. Many have argued that the Archimancer, Fozzrik, was behind the creation of the Floating Village, and there is much evidence to support this theory. It certainly seems reasonable that Fozzrik may indeed have sought to perfect his arcane techniques in such a secluded area, but if the village's tribesmen are aware of its origins, they have yet to reveal them.

Stormhenge

No one knows for sure when, and indeed, how, the ancient structure known as Stormhenge was created. Even the Orcs, prevalent throughout the Badlands, give these concentric henges a wide birth. It is thought by some that the pillars are part of a device that funnels the Winds of Magic, channelling them directly into one host, should they stand on the central column. However, this has never been confirmed, for those few Wizards who have been brave – or foolish – enough to stand upon the central pillar have never survived to recount their experience.

Giant Stomping Grounds

Giants are common the world over; although usually found in highlands and striding the sides of mountains, in the Badlands many Giants have been seen wandering the foothills of the Dragonbacks. Although no one is entirely sure why there is such a dense Giant population in the area, rumours of a break out from the Giant holding pens of the Bloody Hand Tribe about three decades past cannot be discounted as the origin.

The Dragonback Mountains

To the east of the Black Gulf rise the mighty Dragonbacks. A mountain chain that may not rival the Worlds Edge Mountains in size, but is no less dangerous as it is crawling with greenskins, Giants and Trolls. As with many mountainous areas, this was once a realm of the Dwarfs but, like an unstoppable green tide, they were overcome by rampaging Orcs, and so the Dragonback Dwarfs were lost to history.

Morgheim

At the heart of the Marshes of Madness lies the Necropolis known as Morgheim. Once the capital of the Strigoi, Mourkain was founded by Kadon shortly after he fell under the dominion of the Crown of Sorcery. At one point the Strigoi realm reached to the Black Gulf, all controlled from Mourkain. The Orcs were far from happy at being pushed from the ancestral lands and joined together in a great Waaagh! Led by Warboss Garsnag Craktoof, Mourkain was sacked, and the power of the Strigoi broken forever. Now known as Morgheim, the city may no longer exert its control across the Badlands but is still a formidable place of lost power.

The Marshes of Madness

The marshes are avoided by all but the desperate. It is a realm of the Undead and a remnant of a past civilisation, forever cursed when the Crown of Sorcery was discovered on the banks of the Blind

River. It is now a virulent swamp that is shunned by all. Within the marshes lies Morgheim and the insidious Tree of Beards, a testament to the folly of the Dwarfs when they once tried to tame the swamp.

Blight Water

The foetid water that indolently makes its way from the Sour Sea to the Marshes of Madness is not one to come across if you have a thirst. The water is black, putrid and if you don't see a dead animal drifting in it, chances are you will come across one should you follow it for a league or so. However, it is those desperate and foolish enough to have drunk from the Blight Water that have most to fear for the rancid taste hides a deadlier threat – one that will not only cause a slow and inescapable death, but will see the victim rise again as a mindless Zombie.

The Serpent's Fang

As well as countless tribes of Orcs & Goblins, the Badlands have long been home to an assortment of outcasts, criminals and other ne'er do wells. In the dark ruins that litter the landscape, cultists often gather far from the prying eyes of the authorities, practicing their sinister rituals until inevitable betrayal becomes their undoing. The Serpent's Fang was once home to just such a cult, the Cult of the Crimson Serpent, a group of Slaaneshi worshippers who briefly wreaked havoc upon surrounding settlements until a group of itinerant warriors slew them.

The Pillar of Bone

When a storm of magic ravages the land, Arcane Fulcrums rise to meet it, great supernatural pillars from the top of which a mage can attempt to harness the magical energies raging all around. Usually, when the storm abates, the fulcrums crumble away, sinking back into the earth. Sometimes, however, the land is so wracked with sorcery that the Arcane Fulcrum remains long after the storm has passed. The Pillar of Bone is one such structure, a smooth-sided tower seemingly made from solid bone. Although the magic that once howled around its pinnacle has now subsided, a mage who sits atop the tower can still harness a glimmer of that power, scrying the future or plucking lost knowledge from the past.

Skull River

Named not so much for the bones of the dead that litter its river bed, but for the leering skull-headed piranhas that haunt its shores and can strip the flesh from an Ogre in under a minute.

The Slaughter at Wyvern Cliffs

Even to those that have no knowledge of events that gave the Wyvern Cliffs their name, it is perhaps unsurprising to any who learn that there was indeed a Wyvern involved and, yes, there was a slaughter. When one delves a little deeper into the history of that sorry event, it all came about when a sneaky Goblin, Furgit Gutslasha, tried to impress his Orc overlord by climbing Iron Rock and make off with a Wyvern hatchling to present as a gift to his master. Suffice to say that the maternally outraged mother was not impressed, and proceeded to annihilate the entire greenskin tribe. Ironically, it is rumoured that only Furgit himself escaped the ensuing massacre. The escaped Wyverns have roosted in the cliffs ever since.

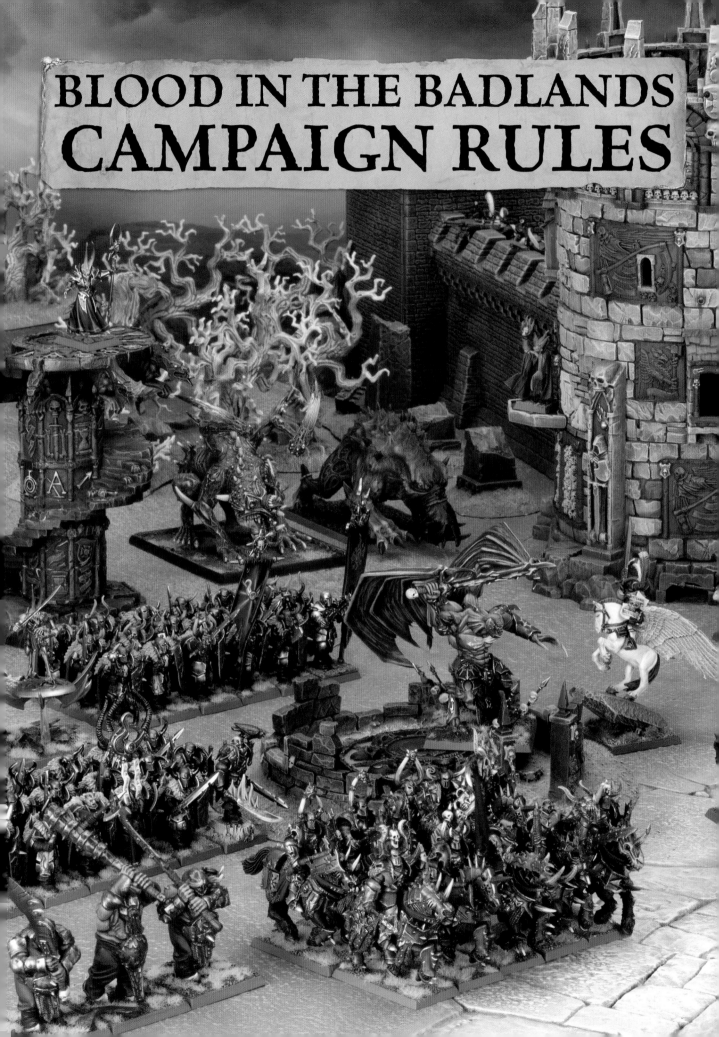

BLOOD IN THE BADLANDS
CAMPAIGN RULES

Heroes and Villains

At the centre of every good story are its heroes and its villains, and a campaign should be no exception. Great fun can be had coming up with characters with their own motivations and plots.

The forces of the Empire want to stop the Flying Fastness falling into the wrong hands.

The hosts of Tzeentch desire Fozzrik's Flying Fastness to sow disorder across the world.

The chittering Skaven greatly covet the warpstone artefacts contained within the fortress.

INTRODUCTION

Blood in the Badlands is an alternate set of campaign rules for use with the Mighty Empires Expansion and Warhammer, centred around the quest for possession of a legendry fortress.

Eight generals have led their armies to the Badlands where they seek Fozzrik's Flying Fastness. A year from now, the castle will touch down somewhere in this troubled land and whoever can seize it will rule victorious.

The surest way to capture the Flying Fastness is to control as much of the Badlands as possible, so that when the fortress lands it will do so within your borders. But that is not the only way to claim the fortress, for the Badlands are littered with ancient ruins containing magical relics. By obtaining as many relics as possible, perhaps a mighty ritual can be enacted and the Flying Fastness stolen by magical means.

The Campaign

The campaign takes place over a year in the Warhammer world, but over the course of 12 turns in the game. In each turn players move their armies, expanding the borders of their empire, build settlements, fortify strongholds and, most importantly of all, wage war. At the end of the campaign the final battle for control of Fozzrik's Flying Fastness is fought, with the victor of the battle winning the campaign.

Fighting the Campaign

Although we wrote these rules to fit the needs of our campaign, we've included them here so that you can fight your own campaign with them. All you will need is a Mighty Empires map (you can find out how we made our map on page 6), some counters to represent armies on the map and a number of players each with their own Warhammer armies.

Pete's Skaven and Chris' Empire clash, the fate of the Badlands at stake.

GETTING STARTED

Creating Characters

At the start of the campaign the first thing each player needs to do is create the hero (or villain) who will lead their empire to war. Each player should come up with a name for their glorious leader and jot down three things about him – something about his description, his personality or his past victories, perhaps. Players should pick their leader as a unit choice too.

Once they've done that, they should come up with a two more named characters to represent his lieutenants.

Armies

Each player starts a season with three armies. Players will need separate counters to track where each one is on the map. Each army represents an expedition led by the leader or one of his lieutenants – note down who is where on an army roster.

As the campaign progresses players might be instructed to remove an army from play – don't worry, the army isn't destroyed but merely scattered until next season.

Heroes of Legend and Regiments of Renown

Many players like to come up with names and background for their characters, champions and units. Although you don't need to do this, it does add to the story.

Similarly, as the campaign progresses, heroes and regiments might perform great deeds and earn accolades. Naming them helps players keep track of special units. We refer to such units as Regiments of Renown and such heroes as Heroes of Legend. Once named, each Regiment of Renown and Hero of Legend must be fielded in exactly the same size and be armed with the same wargear whenever that army fights a battle.

Allies & Enemies

Each player must then decide which of their rival generals is his enemy and which is his ally. They should come up with an explanation for what they have done in the past to earn their enmity or their trust. Aside from a couple of results on the Random Events table, this doesn't have any game effect, but it does help create rivalries and alliances in the story!

Setting up the Map

Roll-off to determine the order of set-up.

Each player then places their capital city and claims the surrounding six tiles as their empire by planting a flag in each. Do this in such a way that each player has seven tiles – no capital city can directly border another empire, although two empires can border one another. They can then place a mine and a fortress anywhere in their empire.

Each player then places their three armies anywhere within their empire.

Finally, the Flying Fastness itself is placed in a random tile and the campaign can begin!

Army Counters

We made counters for our armies by gluing Warmaster characters onto round slottabases, although you could use anything you like.

Matt's magic-heavy Vampire Counts army is represented by this Necromancer.

The army of Faelar Bladestorm, one of Simon's High Elf armies.

Andy used a variety of Warmaster Clanrats for his army counters.

One of Andrew's armies comprises entirely mounted models, as this counter shows.

Tom's Daemon Prince, the Grim Nebula, as represented on the campaign map.

Army Rosters

For each army, you will need to keep track of its general, Heroes of Legend and any Regiments of Renown on an army roster. There is no set rule as to what you should track for each army or how large it is – at the minimum you should know which of your named characters is in charge and what they are armed with. At the opposite end of the scale you might wish to name each of your regiments and their champions. As the campaign progresses and your units and heroes gather accolades, you'll need to note these down too. You can find a blank Army Roster at the end of this book.

Regiment of Renown: The Everwardens												Composition: 17 Chaos Warriors	
Name/Type	M	Ws	Bs	S	T	W	I	A	Ld	Sv	Type	Equipment & Special Rules	
Chaos Warrior	4	5	3	4	4	1	5	2	8	3+	Infantry	Mark of Tzeentch, Shields, Full Command	322
The Dark One	4	5	3	4	4	1	5	3	8	3+	Infantry	Immune to Psychology	
Mount													

Notes & Famous Deeds:
The Everwardens won infamy early in the campaign by holding fast in the face of a mighty Necrosphinx whilst holding a Watchtower until reinforcements could show up and finally finish the beast off.

CAMPAIGN TURNS

In Between Turns

The tale of the campaign is played out both at the campaign map and the battlefield, with great deeds accomplished, victories won and legends forged. But the story doesn't need to end when you put down the dice – it can be fun to write about the exploits of your heroes as they take to the field, as well as to hurl insults and challenges as your rivalries with the other players develop.

When we played our campaign (and indeed, for all of our Studio campaigns) we set up a group email list so that we could write battle reports, issue challenges, gloat about victories and curse the dice gods about defeats. It was via this medium that we discovered Chris Peach's inner poet, as he recorded every game he played as a poem written by the now-infamous Siegfried Schweinsteiger.

We've included much of the correspondence throughout this book, not just to give you a flavour of the campaign, but also to inspire you to write your own missives in between games.

"Squeak squeak." The Skaven messenger squeaked, scraping humbly in front of the Grey Seer. "We have received another... message."

"It better not be what I think it is," replied the Seer, munching on the remains of the last messenger.

"Err, it appears to be from the Man-things." The messenger started to back away cautiously.

"Does it... rhyme?" The Seer stood, his staff in hand.

"It does resemble a poem, my lord."

With a crackle of electricity the message – and the messenger – combusted. If there was one thing guaranteed to spoil the mood of victory it was a verse of poetry.

Turn Order

At each step, each player acts in order of smallest empire to largest before moving on to the next step. Roll-off to resolve ties.

1. Move the Fortress
2. Random Events
3. Move Armies
4. Declare War
5. Roll for Mines
6. Fight Battles
7. Resolve Victories and Defeats
8. Resolve Expeditions
9. End of Turn

1. Move the Fortress

At the start of each turn, Fozzrik's Flying Fastness moves D6 tiles in a random direction. If it hits the edge of the map, it stops and continues its move in a different random direction.

Any battle fought in or adjacent to the tile where the Fortress ends up must be a Storm of Magic battle. In addition, any Storm of Magic battle fought in one of these tiles garners a relic to both players in addition to any other prize.

2. Random Events

Each player rolls a D66 on the Random Events table and resolves the event. Some events affect battles fought during the turn, others only affect campaign actions.

3. Move Armies

The borders of empires are expanded as armies advance across the land. An army can be used to claim unclaimed tiles, fortify lands by building cities, fortresses and mines, fend off invading armies and conquering enemy land.

At the start of each season, starting with the player with the smallest empire, players each place three armies anywhere within their borders. Players take it in turns to move an army one at a time as follows: pick an army, then roll D3 to see how far it moves across the map.

Once a player has moved one of his armies, the next player can do so and so on, allowing players in turn to react to the actions of their opponents.

At least one army must always remain within a player's borders to defend their empire, but they may still move about.

4. Declare War

Starting with the player with the smallest empire, each turn a player can challenge another player to battle, attempting to capture their land or drive off their invading armies. A player may issue one challenge a turn, and may not issue a challenge to an opponent who has already been challenged (unless you fancy playing a three-way game that is). If a player has already been challenged, they may not issue a challenge of their own (unless you want to play more than one game this turn).

The position of armies on the campaign map is crucial to who a player can challenge. When it comes round to your turn to issue a challenge take a look down this list and see whether you fulfil any of the criteria, one by one:

- If you have an army in the same tile as another (non-allied) player, you must issue a challenge to them.
- Otherwise, if another (non-allied) player has an army in your empire, you must issue a challenge to them.
- Otherwise, if you have an army in another (non-allied) player's empire, you must issue a challenge to them.
- Otherwise, if none of these apply, you may challenge any player an ally could challenge instead.

Follow that Fortress
In the example above, the tile shown is nominated to be direction 1. A 3 is rolled, so the fortress moves D6 tiles in that direction.

An Act of War
In the example above, the Tomb King player must challenge the Warriors of Chaos player, as their armies are in the same tile.

Random Events Table

11	*Recalled from War.* Remove one of your armies from play until the start of next season.
12	*Embattled.* Roll 2D3 when moving all your armies this turn and pick the lowest result.
13	*Enemy Sympathisers.* Any fortification saves you have to make this turn are at an additional -1.
14	*Assassin!* Pick one of your Heroes of Legend and immediately roll on the Character Injury table.
15	*Deserters.* Pick any of your tiles and remove the flag.
16	*Plague.* Remove one of your fortresses, cities or mines, but leave your flag in place.
21	*Stoking Unrest.* Pick any of your enemy's tiles (other than their capital) and remove the flag.
22	*Settlers.* Pick an unclaimed tile and plant your flag in it.
23	*Raiding Party.* Pick a rival's tile without a city, fortress or mine in it and plant your flag in it.
24	*Sappers.* Remove one of your enemy's fortresses, but leave their flag in place.
25	*Grab the Gold!* Pick an enemy's mine and plant your flag in it.
26	*Seize the Crown!* Pick an enemy's city (other than his capital) and plant your flag in it.
31	*The Winds of Change.* Move the Flying Fastness again.
32	*Forced March.* Move one of your armies again.
33	*Swift Steeds.* Roll 2D3 when moving all your armies this turn and pick the highest result.
34	*Bad Intelligence.* You can move one of your enemy's armies this turn.
35	*Unfurl the Flag!* One of your units immediately gains a free magical standard, as per result 4 on the Spoils of War table (see page 19).
36	*Regiment of Renown.* One of your units immediately gains veteran status, as per result 5 on the Spoils of War table (see page 19).
41	*Spies.* In your next game you may take a look at your enemy's army list before you pick your own.
42	*Dawn Attack.* In your next game the enemy must roll a D6 for each unit before deployment – on a 1 they do not deploy and enter play as reinforcements instead.
43	*Scouting Force.* In your next game, after both sides have deployed, you may redeploy D3+1 of your units. You also gain +1 to the roll to see who goes first.
44	*It's a Trap!* In your next game, you may pick whether to deploy and go first or second.
45	*Prepared Ambush.* In your next game, you may pick which scenario you play and whether to deploy first or second.
46	*Stacking the Odds.* In your next game your army is 25% larger than your opponent's.
51	*Siege Force.* If you win a battle this turn, you automatically capture your opponent's tile.
52	*Slave Labour.* You can re-roll the dice for one of your mines this turn.
53	*Diplomacy.* Pick an opponent. They may not challenge you this turn.
54	*Infiltrators at Court.* Pick an opponent. You may pick who they challenge this turn.
55	*Secret Tunnels.* You may pick any opponent to challenge this turn, regardless of location.
56	*Blood Sacrifice.* You may force your enemy to re-roll any rolls he makes on the Character Injury table this turn.
61	*Treasure Map.* Gain a relic and place a mine anywhere on the map.
62	*Unwritten Victories.* Pick one of your armies and immediately roll on the Spoils of War table (see page 29).
63	*Treasure Chest.* Gain D3 relics.
64	*Cunning Commander.* For the rest of the turn you count as having the smallest empire.
65	*Bolstered Defences.* Any fortification saves you make this turn are at an additional +1.
66	*Reinforcements from home.* For the rest of the season, you gain an extra army.

Relics

Over the course of the campaign, players will gain relics, whether through victory on the battlefield, delving deeply into their mines or by random chance. Relics represent assorted treasure, artefacts and pages from Fozzrik's grimoire. Relics can be used in several different ways: they can be given to an opponent to keep them from your lands, traded with other players in exchange for hostages, diplomacy and so on. At the end of the campaign, each player adds up their relics (along with a few other things – see p74).

Let it be known that those who lay a hand upon the proud men and women of Nehekhara will be destroyed utterly, their bones burned and their holds salted. So it was that the Nest-lair of Clan Mange was laid low by the Gods of the Desert, whose vengeful spirits emerged into the laboratory and left but one Skaven soul alive to carry news of the price of crossing King Nekhenaten IVth and his kin.

From Campaign Map to Battlefield

In a campaign, the action takes place on the battlefield as well as the campaign map and it's a good idea to remember that when playing. It doesn't take much effort to set up the terrain to match the area of the map you're playing in or to come up with some special rules to represent the events that have taken place, but it can really add to the sense of story. You can even come up with special scenarios to play – we wrote some new scenarios on a few such occasions, such as when Andrew rescued the Red Witch from the clutches of Clan Mange. Pete even came up with a whole set of rules for underground battles.

5. Roll for Mines

Your mines provide you with gold to pay for mercenaries and iron to forge weapons. In this phase roll a D6 for each of your mines and consult the table overleaf. Any additional points generated can be used in any of the games you fight this turn.

6. Fight Battles

Whenever you come to fight a battle, you need to decide where on the map it is taking place – before you play, you and your opponent should nominate a tile to represent this. This will normally be the tile occupied by your armies.

Battles are fought in the same way as any game of Warhammer. However, when setting up the battlefield or picking a scenario, you might like to bear in mind where on the map the battle is taking place, what the aims of the invading army are and so on.

When picking an army for battle, you are restricted in a couple of ways:

- The game may be of any mutually agreeable size.
- You must take any Heroes of Legend or Regiments of Renown that you have written on your army roster for this army.
- If one army is bigger than the other (because of a roll on the Spoils of War or the Mines table), it may not be more than 25% larger than the opponent's.

7. Resolve Victories & Defeats

In the aftermath of a battle, a victorious army may be emboldened and gain great rewards, whilst a defeated army may be routed and demoralised. The victorious player must roll a D6 on the Spoils of War table whilst the defeated player must roll a D6 on the Ignominious Defeats table. Both players must roll a D6 on the Character Injury table for every Hero of Legend that was removed as a casualty during the game as well.

Finally the winner must roll a D6:

- 1-3 the defeated army is driven back a tile towards its own empire (or capital)
- 4-6 the defeated army is removed from play as it scatters for home.

8. Resolve Expeditions

As well as defeating enemy armies, your own armies can launch expeditions to do all manner of things, from conquering enemy tiles to fortifying your empire.

Starting with the smallest empire, resolve each of the armies in turn:

- If your army was driven back by another army it may not do anything else this turn as it is too busy making a retreat.
- If your army is in an unclaimed tile, you may claim it. Stick a flag in it.
- If your army is in a tile occupied by an

enemy army and a battle wasn't fought, roll a D6: on a 1, your army is removed. On a 2-3 your army is driven back a tile. On a 4-5 the enemy army is driven back a tile and on a 6 it is removed.

- If an army is in its own empire, it may build a fortress, a mine or a wizard's tower if there is not one already. Each tile may only have one building, however, if there is already a fortress there you may replace it with a city instead. Each army may only build once per season.
- If your army is in an enemy tile that does not contain any enemy armies, you may attempt to conquer it. The enemy player may attempt to make a fortification save to see if he can garrison his lands in time and stave off the attackers. Roll a D6 and apply the following modifiers:

  - The tile borders your own -1
  - The tile is adjacent to a fortress +1
  - The tile is adjacent to a city +2
  - Your opponent can give you a relic to bribe you to leave you alone. For every relic handed over he gains +1.

If the roll is 6+ the player is successful and the tile does not change hands. If the save is failed, the tile is conquered – remove the enemy's flag and plant your own there instead!

9. End of Turn

Tidy up the board and start the next turn. At the end of each season, players should remove all their armies. At the start of the next season, players should place all three of their armies anywhere in their empire.

Seasons

The campaign year is split into four seasons, each comprising three turns and a climactic event. Each season has a different special rule, and each event has a special battle and rewards for the victors.

Spring: Any dangerous terrain tests are failed on the roll of a 1 or 2, instead of a 1. In addition, any wizards attempting to cast spells from the Lore of Life this season receive a +1 bonus to their casting roll.

Summer: Whenever an expedition is removed from the map for any reason, replace it in an unoccupied tile anywhere in your empire.

Autumn: Any Storm of Magic games played during Autumn grants both players a relic. Any Storm of Magic games played in an adjacent tile to the Flying Fastness is in your empire grant 2 relics instead of 1.

Winter: Roll a D6 at the start of each battle. On a 1-2 a blizzard sweeps over the battlefield and the maximum visibility is reduced to 24"

POST-BATTLE CHARTS

Spoils of War

1 *Living in Infamy.* Tales of the misdeeds of your army spreads amongst the enemy, fostering a burning hatred at the sight of your banner. Whenever this army next fights a battle against your defeated foe, all their units suffer from Hatred.

2 *Elite Army.* The next time you fight a battle with this army, the limits on Special or Rare choices are increased to 75% and 50% respectively.

3 *Ranks Bolstered.* The next time you fight a battle with this army, you may take an additional D6x50 points.

4 *Beneath a Proud Standard.* Pick one of your units and name it as a Regiment of Renown – it may pick a magic standard worth up to D6x10 points for free. Write down which one on your army roster. If the standard is ever lost in battle, scrub it off your list.

5 *Valorous Deeds.* Pick one of your units to be recognised for its valiant efforts and name it as a Regiment of Renown. Roll a D6 to see what special rule it gains: 1 = Devastating Charge, 2 = Armour Piercing, 3 = Always Strikes First, 4 = Immune to Psychology, 5 = Stubborn, 6 = Fear.

6 *The Glitter of Gold!* Not only do you find a relic (add it to your tally), but also a magical artefact. One of your Heroes of Legend may take a magic item worth up to D6x10 points for free (this does not count against his magic item points, but he still cannot take two magic weapons, talismans and so on). Write down which one on your army roster. If the character is ever slain in a challenge, scrub the magic item off your list.

Ignominious Defeats

The defeated army must roll a D6 on the following table:

1 *A Sound Beating!* When your army next fights the race that defeated them, all the enemy units cause Fear.

2 *Walking Wounded.* Pick a unit from the defeated army. It is unavailable to fight this army's next battle.

3 *Understrength.* Pick a unit from the defeated army. It fights at half strength in this army's next battle.

4 *Inexperienced Leaders.* Pick a unit from the defeated army. It has Stupidity in this army's next battle.

5 *Green Troops.* Pick one of your Regiments of Renown that has received Valorous Deeds or Beneath a Proud Standard in the past. It loses this ability/standard.

6 *Vengeance will be Ours!* When this army next fights a battle against the race that defeated you, all your units suffer from Hatred.

Character Injuries

If a Hero of Legend is removed as a casualty in the game, roll a D6 on the following table:

1 *Serious Injury:* Roll again. 1 = Dead!, 2 = -1 M, 3 = -1 WS and -1BS, 4= -1 S, 5 = -1 T, 6 = -1 A.
   If any characteristic is reduced to 0 then the character is too infirm to take part in any further battles, unless their characteristic started at 1, in which case re-roll the result.

2 *Captured!* The enemy have taken him hostage. If they still hold him at the end of a season each hostage is worth 1 relic. To rescue him you'll need to defeat the army that captured him or play a special scenario.

3 *Minor Injury:* Roll as for a serious injury, except that the result only applies in the next battle. In this case Dead is instead Coma, and the character may not be used in the next battle his army fights.

4 *Psychological Injury:* Roll again: 1 = Fear race fought against, 2 = Frenzy, 3 = Hate Race fought against, 4 = Stupidity, 5 = Stubborn, 6 = Immune to Psychology. If the character already has the rule, roll again.

5 *Where's my Sword?* One random magic item owned by the character is lost in the battle. The enemy may roll a D6: on a 6 they can add it to their own roster. Otherwise the item is lost forever!

6 *Heroic Escape!* Not only has he recovered but he is changed by his ordeal and gains +1 to a characteristic – roll to randomly determine which one. No characteristic can be increased to more than 10.

Customising the Cartography

After making our map, we took a look at all the various features and locations and came up with special rules to match them. It's easy enough for you to do the same, tailoring the rules to match your own map. So, for example, if your campaign has a Wood Elf player then you'll want more forests!

Mine

Wizard's Tower

Stormhenge

Hanging Rock

Iron Rock

SPECIAL RULES

Fortress: A fortress adds +1 to the fortification save of any adjacent tiles. In addition, a tile containing a fortress can only be captured if an opponent first wins the Siege scenario.

City: A city adds +2 to the fortification save of any adjacent tiles. In addition, a tile containing a city can only be captured if an opponent first wins a Siege scenario.

Mines: Roll a D6 for each mine you control after you have moved your armies:

1   *Collapse!* The mine is exhausted. Remove the mine.
2-4   *Gold and Iron.* See result 3 on the Spoils of War table.
5-6   *Fabulous Treasures!* See result 6 on the Spoils of War table.

Wizard's Tower: A player with a wizard's tower may reverse the roll on the Random Events table (so a 65 would become a 56). In addition, in any battle fought here all Wizards gain the Loremaster special rule.

Stormhenge: If a player still has a captured hero at the end of a season, they may sacrifice them at the stone circle to gain D3 relics. In addition, for any battle fought here the whole table counts as an Arcane Ruin.

Hanging Rock: The player controlling Hanging Rock may re-roll the roll on the Character Injury table once per turn. In addition, for any battle fought here models using the Lore of Death add a free power dice to their casting attempts.

Iron Rock: The player controlling Iron Rock may include allies chosen from the Orcs & Goblins army book in any game he plays. In addition, for any battle fought here the whole board counts as an Idol of Gork.

Barak Varr: Barak Varr counts as both a city and a fortress that gives a +3 fortification save to the tile it is in and any adjacent mountain or river tiles. It starts in the possession of the Dwarfs.

Morgheim: At the end of the campaign, Morgheim counts as 5 relics. In addition, in any battle fought here the whole table counts as a Charnel Pit. Morgheim is the prize for winning the scenario at the end of summer and may not be claimed till then.

The Marshes of Madness: The marshes have a fortification save of 2+ to represent the difficulties of conquering such a maddening land, but you may never build in them. Each of the Marshes of Madness count as

2 relics at the end of the campaign. The Marshes of Madness are the prizes for winning the scenario at the end of summer and may not be claimed till then.

Mount Bloodhorn: Mount Bloodhorn counts as a mine that can never be exhausted – ignore results of a 1. Mount Bloodhorn also counts as a fortress. At the end of the campaign Mount Bloodhorn counts as 5 relics. Mount Bloodhorn is the prize for winning the special scenario at the end of the spring season and may not be claimed till then.

Fozzrik's Gatehouse: The Gatehouse counts as a wizard's tower and a fortress. At the end of the campaign the Gatehouse counts as 5 relics. The Gatehouse is the prize for winning the scenario and is placed anywhere on the map by the winner.

Racial Rules

Beastmen: Beastmen are driven into a state of fury by the trappings of civilisation. Any tiles occupied by a Beastman army, and any adjacent tiles, do not get bonuses to fortification saves from fortresses or cities.

Bretonnia: Armies of crusading knights ride full pelt across the land seeking the grail. Bretonnian armies add an additional +1 when rolling to see how far they move.

Daemons of Chaos: Daemons of Chaos are immaterial creatures of magic manifest. Before any armies are moved, the Daemon player may move his armies 1 tile in any direction. In addition, once per turn after challenges have been declared the Daemon player may swap the position of any two of his armies.

Dark Elves: The Dark Elves capture slaves to toil in their mines. For every battle won in the previous turn, a Dark Elf player gains +1 to any rolls on the Mine table. In addition, a Dark Elf player counts all coastal tiles as adjacent to your empire, regardless of its true position.

Dwarfs: The mines of the Dwarfs are sturdy and well defended structures. Dwarf mines add +1 to the fortification saves of the tile they are in, and any adjacent tiles.

Empire: The lands claimed by the Empire are garrisoned with serried ranks of State Troops. Empire cities and fortresses provide an additional +1 fortification bonus.

High Elves: The Elves of Ulthuan are swift, their armies moving with great speed.

Whenever moving an army, a High Elf player may re-roll the dice to see how far it moves. In addition, a High Elf player counts all coastal tiles as adjacent to his empire, regardless of its true position.

Lizardmen: Slann Mage Priests scry the future from their Temple-cities. Lizardmen cities also count as wizard's towers.

Ogre Kingdoms: Ogre tribes migrate across the land, never settling in one place for long. The capital city of an Ogre empire can move in the same way as an army, but may not leave the borders of its empire.

Orcs & Goblins: The Badlands are infested with greenskins. Whenever an Orc & Goblin army is removed from the map, replace it in an unoccupied tile anywhere in its own empire.

Skaven: The surface dominions of the Skaven are the tip of the iceberg, their true empire stretching far beneath the surface. Once per turn, a Skaven army may move anywhere on the board instead of moving normally. When resolving expeditions, however, roll a D6: on a 1-2 the army is removed as the cowardly Skaven skulk back into their tunnels. On a 3-4 the expedition is resolved as normal. On a 5-6

the expedition is resolved as normal, but in addition a mine is placed on the tile.

Tomb Kings: Many of the warriors of Nehekhara still lie buried beneath the sands, ready to answer their Tomb King. Once per turn a Tomb King player may remove any one of their armies from play and place it anywhere in their empire. A Tomb King player does not have to leave an army within his empire, so long as he moves an army back if attacked.

Vampire Counts: Animated by powerful necromancy, the Undead are not easily put down. Vampire Counts characters may re-roll results on the Character Injury table.

Warriors of Chaos: The Warriors of Chaos are the masters of conquest and slaughter, readily razing cities to the ground. When a Warriors of Chaos army is conquering a tile, any fortification saves made by the opponent incur a -1 modifier.

Wood Elves: The spirits of the forests are angered by the presence of intruders. Wood Elf players add an additional +1 to fortification saves made for forested tiles. In addition, once per turn one Wood Elf army may move from one forested tile to another, anywhere on the map.

Making it Up

These, then, are our customised set of Mighty Empires rules we used for our campaign. They'll work perfectly well for your campaigns as well. But you don't have to leave it at that – Mighty Empires is designed to be a customisable campaign tool to suit your needs and you're encouraged to come up with your own rules. What you will need is one player to be the campaign Games Master. He is the person who works in the background, making sure games are played on time, coordinating the map moves, rolls for mines, and so on, as well as adjudicating story lines as they evolve as well as settling any differences of opinion. Needless to say, the GM can be a player as well. In our campaign Andrew was the GM as well as forging his own Tomb King empire.

The Dwarfs find that the dead do not rest easily when they attack the empire of the Tomb Kings.

THE DIREHOST

Matt Hutson is more commonly seen fielding an army of Elves, be they of the Dark, High or Wood Elf variety. By starting an army of the Vampire Counts, it seems that he puts little stock in the short-lived mortal races, but immortality has its perks, we suppose.

Lord Morivar Darkstalker
Castellan of Dragon Keep, a lonely tower in the shadow of the Dragonback Mountains, even the local greenskin tribes know to avoid Darkstalker's domain.

Rashiel Direblood
The right hand and, many believe, the consort of Lord Darkstalker, Rashiel Direblood is the general of Dragon Keep's host.

Ervin the Wightmaster
A Necromancer of prodigious power, Ervin is followed at all times by his bodyguard of Wights.

Rashiel Direblood

As soon as Alex Hedström's Zombie Dragon kit was released, I knew that I needed to paint one. When the call then came for players to take part in the Blood in the Badlands campaign, I took it as a sign to turn this beautiful model into the general of a new army. The idea for Vampire Lord Morivar Darkstalker and the Direhost of Dragon Keep was born shortly afterwards, and I began frantically painting a suitable army for him to lead.

Sticking with the Blood Dragon theme, my first addition was a unit of five Blood Knights – between them and my Vampire Lord on Zombie Dragon, they can crush an army almost single-handed! As much as these guys cost a fair few points, I'm confident that they will make such an impact on the battlefield that they will more than justify their inclusion. In fact, I find that such powerful units often distract opponents to such an extent as they desperately try to counter or avoid them, that you can press your advantage and hit their army right where it hurts. Why fight fair when you can fight dirty?

Having allowed myself to get a bit carried away with the more powerful units, I decided that I really ought to crack on with a few Core choices. As a regular player of Elf armies, I'm well aware of the effectiveness of small, hard-hitting units that prey on the enemy's flanks. I therefore plan on fielding small units of Crypt Ghouls, as their 2 Poisoned Attacks each makes them perfect to perform such a role.

With my hunting packs of Crypt Ghouls prowling the flanks, I needed a solid battleline to hold the enemy and allow the Ghouls to do their work. Two large hordes of Skeleton Warriors were the obvious solution, as I intended to avoid paying the points for any Zombies by raising them during the game. These units would be armed with spears to grant them as many attacks as possible – the more casualties you inflict, the lower your attrition rate.

I planned on using Darkstalker's lieutenant, Rashiel Direblood in the majority of my battles, saving my dread Vampire Lord for the big, climactic battles at the end of each season, as seemed fitting.

THE TWISTED FLAME

Tom Hutchings, the Studio's megalomaniac, is rumoured to be the Prophet of an underground Cult of Tzeentch. That he so brazenly favours the Master of Sorcery in his Chaos Warriors army is no doubt a cunning ruse to deceive the Witch Hunters that hunt him.

Mawhrin Skel, the Emberblade

This mighty warrior has campaigned for many generations as mortal man counts them, warring seemingly at random across the entirety of the world, led by the whims of the Changer of Ways.

Life is change, and any who stand in the way of such a basic principle ultimately deserve nothing but contempt.

His loyal followers have seen him struck down in battle before, only to rise triumphant from death, invigorated and changed by his unearthly experiences.

I have long had an affinity with the armies of the Dark Gods, and have at some point or other collected every type of army available to the pantheon of Chaos. Saying that, it had been a long time since I last used an army of Chaos Warriors, and decided to rekindle my love for the Chaos-armoured hard-cases.

Tzeentch has ever been my unholy patron of choice, so I decided to lean the theme of my army heavily towards the god of change, lies and deceit. OK, I admit, I'm a bit of a sneaky blighter at the best of times, so Tzeentch's treacherous ways come naturally to me!

Chaos Warriors are undisputed in their position as the best Core troops in the game. With that it in mind, two units of 18 Chaos Warriors form the foundation of every army I field. This number is both highly effective and conveniently a multiple of Tzeentch's sacred number. The Mark of Tzeentch upgrades their parry saves to a healthy 5+, making them incredibly difficult to overcome in combat and perfect frontline troops.

As far as the look of my army went, I themed their style quite heavily on some of the fantastic concept art from Warhammer: Age of Reckoning. These images are particularly prevalent in the designs of my army banners, and also on my commander, Mawhrin Skel himself – Tzeentch is often referred to as the Raven God throughout the lore of Warhammer: Age of Reckoning.

Speaking of my illustrious leader, I converted him with some extensive kit-bashing, as I really wanted him to have a distinctly unique presence on the battlefield, as is fitting for a Chaos Lord.

The Emberblade is ably assisted in his conquests by his daemonic servant, the Grim Nebula. Having defeated the mighty Daemon Prince in a contest of will, he has since bound the ancient creature to fulfil his every capricious whim. As a Lord of Tzeentch, it is of little surprise that Skel commands a powerful sorcerer to do his bidding. Whether or not Ifrit Skybound struck an unholy pact with the Emberblade, or was instructed by Tzeentch to join Skel's host during a vision still remains a mystery.

Mawhrin Skell

THE RATMEN OF CLAN MANGE

Andy Hall is the Studio's most notorious Skaven player. However, with a propensity to roll a 'misfire' every time he picks up an artillery dice, perhaps Andy isn't always suited to fielding the rat-men, where random effects and misfire charts are the norm.

With two Skaven players in this campaign, I was keen for my force and the motives of my leader to be distinctive. Step forward the Screaming One, a particularly evil and cunning Vermin Lord (in, let's face it, a race of especially evil and cunning creatures). Normally, a Vermin Lord, due to his monstrous status, cannot lead a Skaven force. However, as I'd given a compelling reason why the Screaming One was the mastermind behind my army's presence in the Badlands, my fellow campaigners allowed me to use the insidious Vermin Lord as my general.

Each of us had not one but three army commanders, so while the Screaming One would take overall command, he was supported by his 'trusted' lieutenants. They were: Hallscrurry, a Warlord who holds great sway within Clan Mange, currently labouring under the false assumption that should his Daemonic Overlord attain its goal he will be justly rewarded; and Rezziqueak, a Warlock Engineer and Clan Skryre's representative, who are bankrolling Clan Mange's operation in the Badlands.

With my main characters in place it was then time to take stock of my army in preparation for the campaign. I've owned a

The Screaming One
Known as the Screaming One, the vociferous Vermin Lord has forced its way into the mortal realm for thirteen cycles of Morrslieb. Since its arrival, the Rat Daemon, has taken control of Clan Mange and set them to work gnawing through the roots of the Badlands. The Daemon's goal is to hold dominion over the region and therefore enter the ensorcelled castle unopposed, for within lies the Libus Daemonican, a tome that lists the true names of the thirteen-hundred most powerful Daemons. Such knowledge would make a mere mortal powerful beyond measure, but if the tome should fall into the possession of a Vermin Lord… Well, the consequences are too terrible to contemplate.

Skaven army ever since my earliest forays into the hobby, but last year, I decided to start afresh. Taking advantage of the influx of Skaven plastic kits being released, including the Island of Blood, as well as being roped into the latest incarnation of a Tale of Four Gamers, I collected and painted Clan Mange. I used a dark green and off-white colour scheme, and let the Citadel Washes do a lot of my shading and highlighting for me – blessed be to the Horned Rat for the creation of Devlan Mud! With the advent of the campaign I hit the paint station once more. For starters, I obviously needed a Vermin Lord, and so I painted one especially for the campaign. I also treated myself to all the cool new kits that had been released after the 'Four Gamers' series had finished. So, a Hell Pit Abomination, a Plagueclaw Catapult and a Warp Lightning Cannon were added to Clan Mange's growing horde.

I confess to not having a game plan or overall strategy for the campaign. I do plan to forge an early alliance with my fellow Skaven player, Pete, and then hopefully betray him before he inevitably stabs me in the back during the latter stages. I'm going to try and claim as much easy territory as possible. Although I'll shy away from fighting the Dwarfs, above ground at least, as I'm frankly too scared of Kev's super-accurate Dwarf artillery. Snatching as much undefended territory as possible will hopefully leave me with a large empire when the Flying Fastness finally lands.

On the battlefield, I'll lead with my Hell Pit Abomination. With the enemy distracted by this mighty beast, my infantry should be able to strike relatively intact. When my Vermin Lord enters the fray, it'll be to cast the Dreaded Thirteenth Spell over and over, until there is nothing but Clanrats on the table… and beyond!

DEFENDERS OF BECHAFEN

Chris Peach is something of a glutton for punishment. No sooner had he finished painting enormous quantities of Empire infantry to expand the burgeoning Studio army, he proudly announced that he would be painting another such army for this campaign!

Stiegfried Schweinsteiger

Hero of the Three Towers, Saviour of Bechafen, Destroyer of the Fell-kin and chosen of the Emperor. He's a maverick, but by Sigmar he gets results.

Few know of this man's origins – some say he was carved out of pure adamant from the Middle Mountains, others that he knows every Daemon's middle name. Whatever they say, he's Stiegfried Schweinsteiger and woe follows in his wake.

Günter von Hundhausen Stiegfried's trusted advisor, friend and captain. From Bechafen in Ostermark, this valiant warrior will follow Stiegfried wherever he goes. None can break the bond that exists between the two heroes of the Battle of Bechafen.

Wolfgang Lichtmeister An acolyte of light that forever plagues Schweinsteiger's footsteps. His persona is depressing, his features distressing, but the Wind of Hysh within him is strong. And every soldier knows that to fight the darkness, you need to keep strange company.

The Men of the Empire are the true bulwark against Chaos. In a world full of horrors, Daemons and magic, much of which they have very little understanding, they exemplify a courage and tenacity that arguably rivals that of the Dwarfs – they aren't as powerful or as skilled in battle, but they will face down their enemies nonetheless!

I decided to paint my army as belonging from the eastern provinces of Ostland and Ostermark, as it gave me the opportunity to field an army with plenty of colour and contrast. Another advantage is that the majority of the Empire army is now available in plastic, so it would lend itself to plenty of kit-bashing throughout the army. I always like to personalise each of my armies in order to give it a unique look.

Halberdier regiments form the backbone of the Empire, and for this reason, I never leave home without at least a unit or four. When fighting in horde formation, they greatly benefit from so many Strength 4 attacks and only the most powerful enemy units can hope to engage

them without suffering heavy losses. Depending on which army I am fighting against, I will switch between fielding large infantry blocks, or supporting smaller Halberdier regiments with detachments of Handgunners and Swordsmen.

Black powder weaponry is one of the greatest strengths of the army, and I regularly field a Helblaster Volley Gun and a Great Cannon or two. The Helblaster in particular really helps me to control the battlefield, as my opponents often try to avoid it at all costs, or become so fixated on destroying it that they make mistakes I can pounce on. I'm also a massive fan of Pistoliers, preferably in a ten-man unit, as they hit surprisingly hard for their points.

My secret weapon is, of course, my glorious general, the mighty paragon of poetry that is Siegfried Schweinsteiger, an indomitable duellist and much revered hero of the Empire. That's a pretty impressive reputation to live up to, so I can only hope he does me proud! I'm sure he will, but we'll have to see – a warrior-poet of such renown couldn't possibly fail me, could he?

THE BLADES OF ULTHUAN

Simon Grant has been fielding the Asur in battle for as long as he can remember. Not usually known for taking the subtle approach in battle, Simon is rumoured to use such outlandish concepts as 'manoeuvring' and 'tactics' when using his High Elves. How odd.

Prince Aurelian
When rumours of Fozzrik's Flying Fastness reached the Elven island of Ulthuan, the Phoenix King gave sent forth a fleet to investigate. He gave command to the young, but highly accomplished Prince Aurelian of Yvresse, granting him stewardship of his mighty Dragon Ship, *Indraugnir's Flame*, as a sign of his authority.

Archmage Hothar the Fey
Master of his own floating palace, Hothar the Fey has expressed a professional interest in the secrets empowering Fozzrik's Flying Fastness.

Prince Faelar Bladestorm
A bold warrior renowned as one of the finest swordsmen in Ulthuan.

The High Elves were the first army I collected when I was introduced to the hobby at the tender age of seven. Too many years later, and they're still my favourite Warhammer army. I have been updating my older models with newer, better-painted versions for many years, but the downside of this fanatical obsession is that my army has never truly been finished.

However, a combination of joining this campaign and entering Armies on Parade has seen my High Elves receive more attention than ever before. My army is now on the verge of becoming the grand host of Ulthuan that I've always aimed towards.

I like to represent the kingdom to which each character and unit belongs with a specific spot colour that complements their white clothing. The core of my army has always been from Saphery, and I use a traditional blue as that realm's spot colour: sapphire gemstones, an Asurmen Blue armour wash and Enchanted Blue highlights on the horsetail plumes and armour lining. In a similar way, I use Snot Green as my spot colour for the realm of Yvresse,

Blood Red for Caledor, and Snakebite Leather for the White Lions of Chrace.

On the battlefield, I never leave home without two or three units of Spearmen, as the amount of attacks they can unleash is frightening. I usually field them in units of 28, seven wide and four ranks deep so that all of them can fight if they receive a charge. With the Always Strike First special rule (and usually re-rolling their failed To Hit rolls), they can confidently take on all but the most dangerous enemy units.

As my two lieutenants, Faelar Bladestorm and Hothar the Fey, hail from Saphery, I will be sure to field my large unit of Swordmasters in each of their armies. Not only is this fitting, but Swordmasters are capable of harvesting anything in the game in combat! But I will leave even these deadly warriors behind in my leader's army – as the Herald of the Phoenix King, it only seems right that he will have a contingent of mighty White Lions to act as his bodyguards instead. With my commanders and their regiments of renown in place, the rest of my army is free to remain flexible.

Prince Aurelian of Yvresse

THE ARMY OF THE GOLDEN SCARAB

White Dwarf's esteemed editor, Andrew Kenrick, has been painting his army of Tomb Kings with uncharacteristic devotion of late. Rumours are beginning to circulate that he is in fact obeying the will of his Tomb King, Nekhenaten IV. That would be ironic.

I've always been a fan of the Tomb Kings, ever since they first appeared in the background of the Undead army book. Their fall at the hands of Nagash's treachery and subsequent quest for vengeance across the aeons has always been one of the most iconic tales from Warhammer's background. Yet it wasn't until the release of the latest edition of Warhammer that I had the excuse I was looking for to start a new army.

And so the Great Incantations were intoned and the serried ranks of Naqqara summoned from the tombs. When I started the army, I knew that I was going to paint

plenty of Skeletons – at least a hordes' worth each of Warriors and Archers. Therefore the colour scheme was designed to be as simple to replicate over the whole army quickly and effectively. I was inspired by Paul Dainton's cover to the last Tomb Kings book, with the tarnished bronze armour contrasting with the bleached white of the bone and the whitewashed shields.

I've painted a horde of Skeleton Warriors with spears to form the bedrock of my battleline. I usually put a Tomb Prince or Tomb King in the unit, making them Weapon Skill 5 or 6 and all the more fearsome. I've also painted up a horde of

Skeleton Archers, which can unleash a hail of bowfire at the best of times, and if I can successfully cast *Incantation of Righteous Smiting* on them, they can fire fifty shots a turn! That's gotta sting! One thing I've learned to my cost is not to get my Hierophant killed too easily – she tends to sit in this unit too, behind the frontline but still within range to bolster my army.

With plenty of Core units already under my belt, the start of the campaign proved the ideal opportunity to add plenty of big things to the army – a Necrosphinx, a Khemrian Warsphinx and a unit of Sepulchral Stalkers to be precise. I love the sinister look of the Sepulchral Stalkers – there's something about that impassive bronze death mask that's faintly unnerving. It's for that same reason that I've painted the stone face of the Necrosphinx – it's rather unsettling having a horrific monster topped with an impassive expression on its face.

Originally the army was built around Queen Khalida, and so I wanted my Liche Priests to be a coterie of her handmaidens. Although King Nehkenaten IV now leads the army to battle (at Khalida's behest, no doubt), the handmaidens remain an integral part of my army to this day.

As for King Nehkenaten IV himself, I've used the Tomb King from the back of the Khemrian Warsphinx. He's tooled up for battle, armed with the Blade of Antarhak to allow him to regain lost Wounds, and the Dragonhelm to protect him from any pesky Flaming Attacks – he's rather flammable, after all. You'll notice that I've painted the scarabs on his base gold, to match one of his epithets – the Golden Scarab.

But of course, no army is ever complete, and I'm busy painting up a unit of Necropolis Knights and a Casket of Souls to bolster my spellcasting. Hopefully they'll be ready before the end of the campaign!

King Nekhenaten

In life Nekhenaten IV ruled over the area known today as the Badlands. In death he was interred in the tomb city of Naqqara. In undeath he has returned to reclaim his empire and the ceremonial crown stolen by tomb robbers and sold to Fozzrik to power his great invention. On the battlefield he marches at the head of his glorious army, always surrounded by golden scarabs, the metallic clicking wings of which are often the last thing an enemy will hear.

The Red Witch, the court's Grand Hierophant, constantly whispering advice.

Prince Neher the Bold, more commonly known as the Brash by his men.

THE STORM WARDENS

Artist Kevin Chin's hobby is as relentless as the army he collects. Kevin never turns down a game in the same way that a Dwarf never forgets a grudge. It seems that he has found a kindred spirit in the Sons of Grungni.

Karnji Ravenbeard, The Storm Lord.

The Storm Wardens are responsible for the gathering of intelligence and forewarning of incoming threats. It is their sworn duty to discern credible information to forewarn the Holds, and if possible, to quell the storm before it is even unleashed.

Karnji Ravenbeard is well known for his cunning and battle prowess, yet few know of his more subtle talents, the mastery of which earned him the title of 3668th Storm Lord.

Utilizing surprise tactics, Karnji has often outmanoeuvred his opponents. His tactics are unconventional and risky, yet none can deny his accomplishments. Through sheer grit and wit, Karnji fought his way to victories that many perceive as a lost cause.

Karnji Ravenbeard

The legendary stubbornness of the Dwarfs is something that instantly appealed to me when I began to collect my first army. My first model was Aly Morrison's awesome Daemon Slayer, and since then I've never looked back. The idea of a shamed Dwarf seeking a heroic death in battle armed with the largest axe that he can wield is a wonderful image.

My army heralds from Barak Varr, so I wanted to form my army around a core of Dwarf Rangers, who would be the eyes and ears of the hold, patrolling the coastal approaches and trading routes – the main source of Barak Varr's wealth comes not from mining, but from its trade after all. I prefer to upgrade my Rangers to Longbeards, as their great weapons make them a real force to be reckoned with.

I always field a large unit of Hammerers, the Storm Guard, who act as the personal guard of Karnji Ravenbeard when he leads the army, or the heralds of his will when he is absent. They form the solid, immovable foundation of my army and protect by Battle Standard Bearer at all times. With the Stubborn special rule, Ld 10 and with a re-roll on any failed Leadership tests, these guys will die to a Dwarf before they betray their duty and retreat!

My elite unit of Hammerers are always supported by two large units of Dwarf Warriors. I usually deploy them as a horde, but if they are facing a powerful enemy unit, I will reform them into deep ranks, five wide, as they will likely remain Steadfast and hold up the enemy for as long as it takes to hit them with a counter-charge. I always equip these units with great weapons so they can hit even harder than usual, but also fits nicely with my Longbeard Ranger theme.

Dwarf war machines are simply devastating, and I always take two Cannons and a Grudge Thrower unless I'm too restricted by the agreed points limit. But if I can, I usually take another Grudge Thrower and an Organ Gun as well! I always make sure that I apply the Rune of Fire to my Cannons to take care of any regenerating monsters. Feel the wrath of the Dwarfs, all you Hellpit Abominations out there!

Pete 'the Beard' Foley is one of the country's foremost Warhammer generals, having won the Throne of Skulls, and been in contention for numerous other titles. The Skaven are his current army of choice and his rat-men have terrorised this year's tournament scene. We're not scared. Honest.

Warlord Fawsquikk

Fawsquikk led his forces out of the mountains to escape the yoke of Queek Headtaker and establish his own empire. The enterprising Warlord of Clan Mors found abandoned Skaven tunnels far below the Badlands – a lair from which to begin his quest for world domination… for the Council of Thirteen of course!

Grey Seer Peetsneek
A Grey Seer sent to oversee the movements of Warlord Fawsquikk by the Council of Thirteen.

Grey Seer Itchitt
Peetsneek's litter-kin who appears to aid his brother in the battle against the Dwarfs. He is eternally jealous of his brother's Screaming Bell and plots endlessly to relieve him of its burden.

Brinepox, Priest of the Horned One
A Plague Priest ousted from Skavenblight under mysterious circumstances, seeking to regain his stature and avenge himself on his enemies back home.

I have been playing with Skaven since the new version of the army book was released and have now collected a fairly large army. I am looking forward to using them in this campaign as it isn't often I get to use all my miniatures in a single game. My Warlord is a renowned character in the Studio and I am sure that will lead to a fair few challenges against him during this campaign, especially from my rival, Andy!

His story revolves around leaving Skavenblight to search out an area of the Old World where he can start his own Empire and has settled near the Badlands. When the rumours of Fozzrik's Flying Fastness began to circulate it seemed only right that an ambitious and conniving character like Warlord Fawsquikk would see this as an opportunity to further his own ambitions amongst the Skaven race. But, of course, he will have to contend with Grey Seer Peetsneek peering over his shoulder…

My army centres around the two enormous war machines that the Skaven army can field, the Screaming Bell and the Plague Furnace. These two models make awesome centrepieces for any army of rat-men and my armies will featuring them regularly. Grey Seer Peetsneek's forces will be focused around him on his Screaming Bell and will also include Fawsquikk – he's got to keep an eye on the treacherous Warlord and make sure that he is doing the bidding of the Council of Thirteen, after all!

My other army will include Brinepox riding atop his Plague Furnace surrounded by a fanatical horde of Plague Monks. This unit is a real juggernaut in the game and it can be quite amusing to watch your opponent's forces desperately trying to get out of the way of its unstoppable onslaught.

The final army is led by Peetsneek's twin brother Itchitt. As I have converted a foot model of the Grey Seer off the Screaming Bell kit to play the part of Peetsneek, it seemed right that they would be twins. This army has drafted in a detachment from Clan Skryre and includes all their evil tricks to inflict upon any unwitting foes.

As long as no one betrays him, surely nothing can stop the inevitable victory of Warlord Fawsquikk…

BLOOD IN THE BADLANDS
SPRING

SPRING CAMPAIGN TURN

Annotations

A Fozzrik's Flying Fastness drifts into the skies above Chris' domain.

B Acting like a true Dwarf, Kevin begins to dig deep and build mines throughout his land.

C Simon's expedition up-river clashes with Kevin's rangers, but the High Elves are sent packing and a hasty truce is drawn up between the two.

D Andrew's Tomb Kings march across the border into Tom's empire, but is repulsed by the defenders of the border fort.

E Matt uses his Secret Tunnel event to attack Kevin, but the sortie backfires and ends with Kevin seizing one of his tiles instead. In subsequent turns Kevin would solidified this foothold by building a castle there.

F Both Matt and Andrew uncover a Treasure Chest, gaining 3 and 2 relics respectively.

G Simon strikes south into the land of the Vampire Counts and although his army is victorious Matt holds his tile.

H The pass over the Dragonback Mountains is left haunted after a battle between the Vampire Counts and the Tomb Kings.

I The Skaven capture both Stormhenge and the Red Witch from the Tomb Kings, but Andrew rescues her in time.

Deploying the Empires

As the Badlands' only native empire, Kevin's Dwarfs had to deploy first around their impregnable capital of Barak Varr in the far north. Andrew deployed next, placing the ancient tomb city of Naqqara nestled between the Marshes of Madness and the Dragonback Mountains. Tom deployed next, his empire straddling the length of the Blight Water next to Andrew's lands. Simon went next, claiming the lower reaches of the Black Gulf. Pete deployed his Skaven Under-empire in the mountains north of Tom and Matt claimed the south-west corner of the map. Andy, who had been adamant not to go next to the Dwarfs of Barak Varr, ended up forced into the corner next to Kevin. Finally Chris had no choice but to deploy in the middle!

The onset of spring saw the campaign kick off in earnest. Eight armies converged on the Badlands, heralding a year of perpetual war that would scar the land. Alliances would be struck and broken, and the mettle of each general tested to their limits.

Seasonal Rule

Springtime sees the magical wind of Ghyran blowing strong and the Badlands blooming into life. Trees blossom and flourish and beautiful flowers sprout from the meadows. Not really of course – the Blood Forests grow hungry, the Venom Thickets drip with sickly sweet, poisonous sap and the Marshlands thrive, becoming tangling morasses that are perilous to traverse. And that's not to mention Squig-mating season…

During spring, any Dangerous Terrain tests are failed on the roll of a 1 or 2, instead of a 1, to represent the effect of the overactive wildlife.

In addition, any Wizards attempting to cast spells from the Lore of Life this season receive a +1 bonus to their casting roll.

The campaign began with the arrival of the mighty High Elf Dragon Ship, *Indraugnir's Flame*, weighing anchor in the Black Gulf and sending forth a vanguard army of the Asur led by the battle-hungry Faelar Bladestorm to secure the surrounding region. Bladestorm's host soon came across their ancestral foes – an army of Dwarfs on a long-range patrol from Barak Varr – and the hot-headed Elf Prince attacked without question. A hard-fought and bloody battle saw the High Elves driven back, but at great cost to the Dwarfs. The battered Dwarf survivors retreated to their coastal city to regroup only to find their surrounding settlements coming under sustained attack by the skeletal host of the dread Vampire Countess, Rashiel Direblood bursting forth from hidden tunnels. But it wasn't long before a fresh army of Dwarfs was mustered to drive off the Undead menace. The Dwarfs achieved a crushing victory, and the Countess herself barely escaped the merciless slaughter.

Amidst the increasing tension in the region, rumours began to spread that the Skaven were abroad. It wasn't long before these sightings were confirmed, the Empire army of Günther von Hundhausen learning first-hand as their patrol was ambushed and utterly routed by the skittering swarms of

Clan Mange. Scant days later, the Skaven of Clan Mors were also seen assailing the embattled Dwarfs of Barak Varr. The Dwarfs were soundly beaten, but not before capturing the ratman general, Warlord Fawsquikk, and imprisoning him deep within their impregnable fastness.

However, the Tomb Kings refused to abandon one of their own when Clan Mange captured their Grand Hierophant, the Red Witch, during a vicious battle. The Skaven were preparing to sacrifice the powerful Liche Priestess, but were interrupted at the climax of the ritual by a desperate attack. Fell animated constructs emerged from beneath the gathered Skaven, tearing them asunder and escaping with the Red Witch. But it seemed that the brief absence of their Grand Hierophant affected the performance of the Tomb Kings legions, as they suffered a heavy defeat at the hands of their vampiric rivals on the surface even as they launched their rescue attempt deep below the earth. The Red Witch returned to lead her skeletal host, but before she could return safely to her lands, she came under attack by the Elven Host of Hothar the Fey. The Tomb Kings host was destroyed, but to little avail, as the Red Witch reemerged from the Sea of Souls to take her place of the side of King Nekhenaten once more.

WANTED!

For the theft of a priceless heirloom.

A bounty is hereby posted for the recovery of a priceless gold sarcophagus stolen from the noble empire of Naqqara. Prince Neher the Bold offers up a valuable treasure upon recovery of the sarcophagus, which was very dear to his father, who has sadly gone missing at the same time.

REWARD: A priceless artefact of great importance and unbound power.

In addition, if the Chaos Sorcerer Lord Ifrit Skybound can be delivered to the golden city of Naqqara, dead or alive, the reward shall be doubled!

REWARD: The output of Naqqara's mines for one whole turn.

– Andrew's email seeking the return of his captured Tomb King.

Lord of the Sword

Having settled his differences with Kevin's Dwarfs in the face of their common enemy (for the time being at least), Simon set about avenging Matt's attack on Barak Varr to honour this new alliance. In a tense battle fought over a foetid charnel pit that greatly strengthened Matt's army, Faelar Bladestorm proved his superlative skill as a swordsman, striking down Matt's Vampire Lord in a challenge and securing a great victory for Simon's High Elves.

*He flew to battle upon his steed,
To fulfil his honour-bound deed.
He charged up towards the hill,
To confront his chosen kill.*

*The hordes of Chaos laughed with jest,
For a single man approached their nest.
Dressed for war, a man of the Empire,
For this was Stiegfried Schweinsteiger.*

*Of the Daemon's size he was one tenth,
Yet undeterred he gathered his strength.
They both saluted with magical swords,
For this would be a duel between lords.*

*They fought for hour after hour,
Man versus abyssal tower.
The ringing sound of blade upon blade,
This was the day a hero would be made.*

*His sword struck the beast's chest,
For this man was trained by the best.
The creature sprayed arterial blood,
That ran down the hill like a flash flood.*

*The abomination turned to run,
But Schweinsteiger was not yet done.
The Daemon fell, a bloodied wreck,
As his head was severed at the neck.*

*With blade, song and ancient curses,
This man had wrought bloody verses,
And for his people he did show it
That Schweinsteiger is a warrior poet!*

– Chris' poem to honour his general's heroic victory against Tom's mighty Daemon Prince.

Treachery and Diplomacy

The Chaos Sorcerer, Ifrit Skybound, led Tom's Chaos horde in defence of his homeland, destroying the invading army of Andrew's Tomb King, Nekhenaten IV. Ever one to keep an ace up his sleeve, Tom decided against sacrificing Andrew's defeated general, but instead bound him within his ancient sarcophagus and held him captive. Time proved him wise, as Tom's next game saw his Daemon Prince at the mercy of Stiegfried Schweinstieger after being challenged to a duel by Chris' leader. A combination of trickery and diplomacy saw Tom secure the Daemon Prince's release, Chris accepting King Nekhenaten in exchange for sparing the Daemon's life. Andrew wasted no time in striking a deal for the return of his general, exchanging a 'priceless' artefact for his freedom – a 5-point Ironcurse Icon. Andrew could no longer select this item, and Chris could now include it for free!

SPRING SCENARIO
THE SIEGE OF MOUNT BLOODHORN

The multi-player battle that will see out the spring season is to be decided at the gates of the abandoned Dwarfen stronghold of Ekrund on the slopes of Mount Bloodhorn. Campaign map tiles, magic items and relics are all be up for grabs.

Mount Bloodhorn

The mightiest peak of the Dragonback Mountains, Mount Bloodhorn towers above the surrounding land like a vast monolith of terrifying magnitude. But the mountain's majestic appearance belies its fell reputation – Mount Bloodhorn has long been the spiritual home to the many tribes of greenskins that dwell in the Badlands. Few adventurers dare to travel beneath the mountain's shadow, and fewer still brave the perilous trail up to the abandoned mining settlement of Ekrund, despite persistent rumours of the treasures that lie within. But recent events have drawn the warring armies of the Badlands to the very gates of the stronghold to stake their claim.

As spring draws to a close and the days grow longer, so too are the encamped armies of the Badlands growing restless. After many long months of war, each side looks to new strategies to claim the upper hand in the fighting yet to come. But rumours abound of great treasures abandoned by the Dwarfs as they retreated from the greenskins during the sacking of Ekrund long ago – treasures that may help to turn the tide as the summer campaigning season draws near…

Scenario Special Rules

This scenario is designed for two teams each of three players or more. It is played simultaneously on three separate battlefields: Stonemine Tower, Bitterstone Mine and the Gates of Ekrund.

Each player chooses his force using the army list from a Warhammer army book, to an equal points value agreed before the game. If playing as part of the campaign, each player should use his leader or one of his lieutenants, and any combination of Heroes of Legend and Regiments of Renown from any of his army rosters – such a key battle demands the attention of their empire's finest warriors, after all.

Before forces are deployed, each team must secretly decide which of their players will fight on which battlefield. More than one army can fight on each battlefield, but an army may not be split up between several battlefields. The rules for allies should be used where more than one army is fighting on the same battlefield. If a team wishes, it can choose to contest only one of the battlefields, although this is an unwise strategy! If any of the three battlefields is uncontested, the team that did contest it count as winning that game automatically.

The games on all three battlefields should be played simultaneously, but players need not wait for the same turn on each table to be completed before continuing. This is intentionally lenient in order for each game to flow nicely, but it helps to try and play at a steady pace.

Attackers and Defenders

Before the scenario begins, players should determine which team is attacking Mount Bloodhorn and which team is defending – this can be by mutual consent, by a roll-off, or might be dictated by events in the campaign. When we played this game, the Forces of Destruction were the defenders.

THE GATES OF EKRUND

The Gates of Ekrund is the main battlefield, and victory here determines the overall winners of the scenario. This battlefield uses the Siege scenario from page 88 with the following exceptions:

The Battlefield

The Gates of Ekrund are built into the very mountainside itself. To represent this, deploy two Mighty Fortresses in the corner of the board.

The Relief Force

The defenders do not have a relief force as normal. Instead, both sides may gain receive relief forces depending on the outcome of the other games.

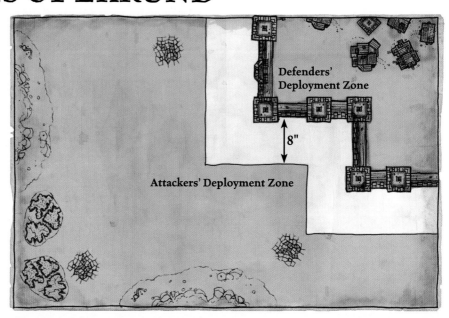

Defenders' Deployment Zone

8"

Attackers' Deployment Zone

STONEMINE TOWER

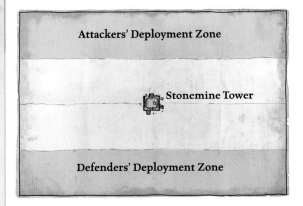

Stonemine Tower guards the approach to the Gates of Ekrund. Victory here determines whether the besieged team can get their relief force through in time before the walls are breached. This battlefield uses the Watchtower scenario.

Control of the Watchtower
The team that are defending Mount Bloodhorn are in control of the watchtower at the start of the battle. The attacking team will therefore receive the first turn as per the scenario rules.

The Gates of Ekrund – Relief Force
As soon as the game ends, the victorious side (attackers or defenders) may relieve the forces fighting over the Gates of Ekrund. Any surviving models on the victorious side may arrive on the Gates of Ekrund board at the start of the next friendly turn, exactly as described for the Relief Force in the Siege scenario.

However, any wounds and casualties received during this battle are carried over to Gates of Ekrund board, as the army has had no time to rest.

BITTERSTONE MINE

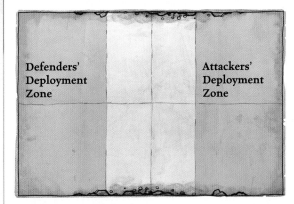

The tunnels of Bitterstone Mine run deep beneath the fortress. Victory determines whether sappers can lay low the mighty walls. This battlefield uses the Battle for the Pass scenario and the underground rules.

Subterranean Intervention
As soon as the game ends, the victorious side may launch a counter-attack against the enemy forces at the Gates of Ekrund. If the attackers won, they may immediately roll two D6 for each of their surviving units, re-rolling rolls of a 6. Each re-roll of 1-3 immediately destroys a defending war machine. Each re-roll of 4-6 breaches a wall section of their choice.

If the defenders won, they may immediately roll 2D6 for each of their surviving units. Each roll of a 6 destroys one attacking war machine, siege tower or other such siege equipment (with immediate effect).

In addition, follow the rules for the relief force (see left), but arriving from the long table edge adjacent to the fortress. Relief units may arrive inside the castle if their team have breached or occupy a wall or tower section adjacent to the board edge.

TO THE VICTORS THE SPOILS

Once the Siege of Ekrund has been decided, one player on the winning side must be declared the overall victor, who will win the greatest share of the prize. The overall victor is chosen by the players on the losing side, who will decide which of the winning generals most contributed to their side's victory. The treasures of Ekrund are divided as follows:

Campaign Map Tile & Magic Items
The player declared the overall victor at the end of the game receives the Mount Bloodhorn campaign map tile. The other players on the winning side must share out the following magic items to add to one of their armies (roll off to see who gets first choice):

The Shield of Ekrund
Magic Armour
This battered shield is rumoured to have belonged to Osrik the Indomitable, the last of the Ironbreakers to fall defending Ekrund.

Shield. When wielded with a hand weapon, this shield gives the bearer a 5+ parry save.

The Banner of Mount Bloodhorn
Magic Standard
The crude stitching and daubed tribal markings identify this tattered banner as being of greenskin origin, and echoes of their bloodlust and aggression remain bound to its fabric.

Models in a unit with the Banner of Mount Bloodhorn gain the Devastating Charge special rule the first time they charge in each game.

The Icon of the Siegebreaker
Magic Talisman
The Runesmith that forged this pendant believed that as long as he wore it, the walls of Ekrund would never be breached. He must have forgotten it on the day Ekrund fell.

When fighting a Siege scenario, you may re-roll all the dice when rolling for Attacking or Defensive Artillery Fire.

Relics
Every player who participates in the Siege of Mount Bloodhorn received D3 relics, whether they win or lose.

BATTLE FOR THE TOWER

This battle promised to be a boney affair, as Andrew's Tomb Kings would be facing off with Matt's Vampire Counts for control of Stonemine Tower. As the defender, Matt was able to claim the watchtower with a small unit of Crypt Ghouls as both players deployed their armies, but Andrew would go first.

He immediately sent his Tomb Guard, led by King Nekhenaten IV himself, charging into the Crypt Ghouls holed up in the tower, but they were repulsed by the flesh-eaters. Matt took ruthless advantage of this turn of events, and sent a summoned Spirit Host to hold them up for what turned out to be the rest of the game!

Matt pulled off a similar trick against Andrew's Necropshinx, bogging it down with a seemingly endless tide of Zombies. For every one the mighty war statue cut in half, another five Zombies would crawl out of the ground – Stonemine Tower had obviously been the site of many battles, as corpses were in an endless supply.

The Skeleton Chariots crashed through the Crypt Ghouls as they emerged from the watchtower, but their rampage was halted by the implacable Grave Guard and their Wight King. Matt occupied the tower with Rashiel Direblood and her Skeleton horde, and held it for the remainder of the game.

Going Out with a Bang!

Matt's Blood Knights carved a bone-strewn path through the Skeleton hordes, smashing them apart before they could assault the tower. Crashing through Andrew's broken lines, they charged headlong into the Casket of Souls that had been causing Matt so much trouble during the battle. The Blood Knights destroyed it in short order, but in their moment of triumph, Matt's seemingly unstoppable cavalry were consumed in white light and slain as the tortured souls bound within the Casket of Souls were unleashed!

TERROR UNDERGROUND

This underground battle rather appropriately featured Dwarfs and Skaven, with Kevin's warriors facing off against Andy's skittering hordes. As they would be playing the Battle for the Pass scenario, both players set up lengthways, with Kevin taking advantage of his generous deployment zone to set up as far back as possible to get the most from his artillery.

And he did just that, unleashing some punishing salvoes from his Grudge Thrower and two Cannons, blasting great chunks out of Andy's units and felling his Hell Pit Abomination. Kevin complemented this bombardment with a cunning ruse, attacking from behind Andy's line with some Dwarf Rangers to disrupt his advance.

Andy fought back, using the powerful magic of his Vermin Lord to soften up Kevin's large infantry units (see right) before sending in the Rat Ogres to finish them off in combat. The giant, mutated beasts slaughtered an embattled unit of Dwarf Warriors before breaking through Kevin's lines and falling upon the war machines that were causing so much damage.

But Kevin's artillery and sneaky Ranger attack had already done enough by the time the Vermin Lord and Rat Ogres made their presence felt, and Andy couldn't stop the Dwarf Hammerers from winning the day.

Chosen of the Horned Rat
Having held his Vermin Lord back for the first few turns to avoid Kevin's artillery, Andy's general finally emerged from cover to threaten the big unit of Hammerers. Andy slew half of them with the *Curse of the Horned Rat* before repeating this devastating spell on Kevin's large unit of Dwarf Warriors the following turn. But Kevin was more upset about Andy's Vermin Lord surviving no less than four cannonball hits by passing his 5+ ward save during this period of time!

THE SIEGE OF EKRUND

After laying siege to Ekrund for many days, the combined army of High Elves and Men of the Empire prepared their final assault on the walls. Defended by an unholy alliance of Chaos Warriors and Skaven, the battle promised to be a bloody one.

Annotations

A Chris' Great Cannons maintain a steady bombardment on the walls with their Siege Ammunition...

B ... but to Kevin's horror, a wayward cannonball overshoots its target and destroys an ancestral statue! Kevin vowed to avenge this slight on the Dwarfs at a later date. But no matter how long it took, he would not forget.

C The only surviving Siege Tower crashes into the eastern tower, delivering its cargo of Empire Halberdiers into the fray, who sweep the ramparts clear of villainous rat-men.

D As the Grim Nebula sweeps down from the battlements in a bid to delay the lethal Swordmasters. In the face of such evil the High Elves' courage betrays them and they flee before combat is even joined.

E In the wake of the fleeing Swordmasters, the monstrous warbeast emerges from the gate and proceeds to tear through everything in range.

F Having tasted defeat in their fateful encounter earlier in the season, the Grim Nebula flees from the glorious charge of Stiegfried Schweinsteiger – the warrior-poet!

The opening bombardment of the battle saw Chris' Great Cannons smash the Hellcannon from the tower ramparts and breach the castle wall in front of Simon's Spearmen. But in return, Tom and Pete managed to bring down two siege towers and wreck a battering ram by sallying forth.

In the wake of this destruction, Simon and Chris threw their forces at the fortress walls and pounded the gate with cannon fire in preparation for an assault by Simon's large unit of Swordmasters. The attack began well, with two units of High Elf Spearmen storming the breached wall section and the adjoining tower, driving Pete's Skaven before them. But Chris' Halberdiers and Greatswords were faced with fierce opposition in the form of Tom's

Chaos Warriors and Pete's Stormvermin, and each wave of attacks was hurled back.

Emerging from the fortress gates, the Hell Pit Abomination tore through everything in its path – Simon and Chris' forces were in such disarray from the Grim Nebula's charge the turn before (see right), that there was little they could do to oppose its blood-fuelled rampage. Their luck began to change when the Dwarf reinforcements arrived, though Kevin's army was denied the option to emerge from inside the fortress walls, as Pete had turned Simon's unit of Spearmen in the tower into Clanrats the turn before!

But the final blow came when Matt's Vampire Counts emerged from the northern table edge and drove the remaining High Elves from the walls to secure the fortress.

A Terrifying Proposition

Simon's deadly unit of Swordmasters were closing in on the fortress gates, and Pete's Skaven were already starting to squirt the musk of fear in apprehension of their attack. Even the Hell Pit Abomination seemed to stall its advance as it emerged from the gates. In a bid to hold them up and delay their assault for another turn, Tom sent the Grim Nebula swooping down from the walls towards Simon's elite unit.

But against the odds, the sight of such a primordial horror coming for their souls caused the Swordmasters to fail their Terror test and flee. Tom and Pete, already in fits of laughter, could barely contain themselves when Chris' Halberdiers also fled in Panic!

Annotations

G The victorious Dwarfs emerge from their subterranean battle with the Skaven, moving on from the western board edge and finally bringing down Pete's rampaging Abomination.

H The men of the Empire cheer as further reinforcements arrive in the guise of the men of Stirland, though all is lost as their true nature is revealed – a shambling Undead horde raised to serve their dread Vampiric master.

BLOOD IN THE BADLANDS
SUMMER

Annotations

A After winning the end of spring scenario, Pete claims Mount Bloodhorn for the Skaven.

B Andy's Skaven emerge from their tunnels to capture two tiles from the High Elves, who fail to stem the tide of invading rats.

C Both Tom and Andy raise extra armies.

D Andrew's Liche Priests raise Swift Steeds, allowing Andrew's armies to roam further.

E Armies of Skaven, the Empire and Warriors of Chaos converge on Stormhenge, eager to capture it for their own ends.

F Matt's general, Morivar Darkstalker, pushes further into the Tomb Kings' territory. Andrew uses his racial special rule to recall one of his armies to defend his land.

G The tomb city of Naqqara comes under siege from the Vampire Countess Rashiel Direblood, but the invading army breaks upon the golden walls.

H The Red Witch leads her army into the heart of a storm of magic, clashing with Hothar the Fey.

I Matt uses his Grab the Gold event to seize one of Kevin's mines, animating the corpses of Dwarfen miners to hew the precious metal for his own coffers.

Expanding Empires

The summer seasonal rule was that if an army was destroyed, it simply reappeared anywhere in its empire. The players really took advantage of this – especially Tom and Matt – pushing their armies far and wide to seize unclaimed and undefended territory. Tom was particularly helped in this matter by the arrival of reinforcements from the Realm of Chaos, gifting him a fourth army with which to expand his empire. With both Pete and Kevin having far-flung footholds amidst the empires to the south, and Matt seizing a mine in the middle of the Dwarfen empire, there were more clashes than in the spring. Andy struck into the heart of the High Elven empire too, using his racial special rule to emerge anywhere on the map.

Following their defeat on the slopes of Mount Bloodhorn, the leaders of the Forces of Order withdrew to their strongholds to lick their wounds and reconsider their alliances. Blood would be spilled in the Badlands anew this summer.

Seasonal Rule
Summer means only one thing in the Badlands – war! The baggage trains are loaded high, weapons sharpened and armour polished as the expeditions march forth to take advantage of the long summer days.

During summer, whenever an army counter is removed from the map for any reason, replace it anywhere in your own empire.

"Know ye, that all who gaze upon these golden gates shall tremble with fear.

All those who set foot upon these stone walls shall cower with terror.

And all those who would do this city harm shall falter and fall."

– Inscription on the (still-standing) Gates of Naqqara

The defeat at Mount Bloodhorn put a strain on the hitherto strong alliance between the Dwarfs and the Empire. Desperate to breach the walls of the wretched citadel, the Empire Engineers had unleashed their artillery, bombarding it with cannon and rocket. Yet the walls were Dwarfen made, for this was once the proud hold of Ekrund, and Lord Karnji Ravenbeard took exception to the handiwork of his ancestors being so carelessly blown apart. Eager to spare bloodshed amongst the former allies, Schweinsteiger challenged the Storm Lord to a duel. Confident that he could best the manling, Kanji was dismayed to be beaten, prompting him to shave his head and take the Slayer Oath.

On the northern shore of the Black Gulf an expedition of Skaven emerged beneath the ancient Elven ruins. The first that Prince Aurelian knew of the invaders was when the silver mines fell silent, dispatching his loyal companion Faelar Bladestorm to investigate. Yet even the Blademaster could not stay the Skaven tide, and his force was overwhelmed and the High Elf had the ignominy of being transformed into a rat by the sorcery of the Vermin Lord.

Far to the south the Vampire Counts were on the move under the cover of darkness, their skeletal legions streaming through the haunted mountain passes to lay siege to the Tomb King city of Naqqara beyond. King Nekhenaten IV himself stood guard atop the golden gates, his Skeleton hordes repulsing three waves of accursed Undead warriors. Although the eastern tower fell to Crypt Ghouls attacking from beneath, the Grave Guard that poured through the breach in the wall were driven back by a charge of Ushabti. The siege was lifted as dawn threatened, and the defenders of the gates named the Lions of Naqqara in honour of their defiance.

As Nekhenaten IV defended his homeland, his Grand Hierophant, the Red Witch, led her own army into battle against the High Elves of Hothar the Fey as a storm of magic swirled overhead. Despite their potent magic, the Elves of Ulthuan were bested at their own game by the ancient incantations of Nehekhara, Hothar the Fey himself consumed in unholy flames atop his Arcane Fulcrum.

Continuing the torment of the manlings, Ifrit Skybound took advantage of the storm of magic that swirled in the wake of Fozzrik's Flying Fastness to siege the border keep. Neither the brave men of the Empire nor their sturdy stonework could stand in the face of the warping power of Chaos unleashed and the castle fell to Ifrit.

The Battle at Stormhenge

As the summer wore on, three expeditions converged on Stormhenge, which lay on the edge of the lands of the Tomb Kings. As Tom, Chris and Andy all desired the territory for themselves, they decided to play a three-way game, using the Battle Royale scenario (Warhammer page 406) with the central pillar as the lone objective. Although both the Skaven and Warriors of Chaos started out nominally on the same side, both turning on Chris' Empire, this truce was never going to last long. Sure enough, Tom 'accidentally' allowed a *Chain Lightning* to leap from Chris' models to Andy's, although he would claim that it was Andy's *Warp Lightning* that was the first hint of betrayal. Despite this treachery, the ruins looked to be safely in the paws of the Skaven until the stalwart state troops of the Empire held firm and the Stormvermin squirted the musk of fear. The Warriors of Chaos took advantage of the rout and marched into the centre, claiming Stormhenge for their own nefarious schemes.

> The mine is mine-mine. Many Elf-things died-died. We chittered.
>
> All hail the mighty Screaming One.
>
> – Andy's declaration of victory over Simon's High Elves

Duels in the Deep

At the start of summer, Andy moved the army led by the Screaming One across the map and into Simon's territory. Simon sent his favoured champion, Faelar Bladestorm, to drive them out. Battle was joined in the depths of Simon's silver mine but the battle proved ill for the High Elves, however, as what the Skaven didn't scorch or zap with magic were consumed by the Abomination. In the aftermath, Faelar sought to reclaim his honour, challenging the Screaming One to a duel. But the Vermin Lord had no qualms about employing deceit, and promptly turned the Elf into a Clanrat. Squeak!

> *To the accursed Nekhenaten IV,*
>
> *Coward I name thee, creature! I blame myself for ever agreeing to such villainous abominations being given the honour of supporting my glorious host. Your lack of presence on the field was beyond forgiveness, and many of my noble brethren died in the siege. These brave heroes sacrificed themselves on the altar of war, but will not return to life, unlike your fiends. Blood begets blood and I challenge thee to battle for the honour of my fallen kin. Prepare yourself, fiend, for a death from which even you will not return.*
>
> *Prince Faelar Bladestorm*
>
> – Simon apportions blame after his defeat at Ekrund.

SUMMER SCENARIO
AT THE MARSHES OF MADNESS

Summer would end as it had begun – in bloodshed. As the armies descend on the Marshes of Madness, so too do their soldiers succumb to insanity as ally turns on ally in the depths of the foetid swamp.

The Marshes of Madness

The southern limits of the Badlands are defined by a great stretch of festering swampland. This area is rightfully known as the Marshes of Madness, for the tainted waters can drive a man insane with but a sip from their stagnant depths, and the mists rising from the marshes can turn friend against friend. Few who venture into the Marshes of Madness return in one piece, for not only is the terrain maddening but its depths are filled with all manner of dangerous creatures. At the dark heart of the Marshes of Madness lie the ruins of Morgheim, a wretched and ruined city that long ago fell to corruption and treachery. Yet for those brave enough, glory and fortune awaits.

As the summer wears on, the putrid swamps of the Marshes of Madness grow ripe with disease and decay, their stench carrying north across the Badlands. 'Tis said that the only reward to be found within the marshes is insanity or death, yet that is not entirely true – much treasure can also be found there.

The Armies

This scenario is for an even number of players, each playing a random opponent. Each player chooses his force using an army list chosen to an equal points value agreed before the game. If playing as part of the campaign, each player should use any of his Heroes of Legend and Regiments of Renown from any of his army rosters.

The Battlefields

Set-up a battlefield for every two players, plus an additional one for Morgheim.

Each battlefield represents an area of the Marshes of Madness, so marshy terrain and foliage should be in abundance.

The additional battlefield should be set-up with a centrepiece of some kind rising out from the misty swamp – a Temple of Skulls is great for this, as is an Arcane Ruin or Dreadstone Blight atop a large hill.

Deployment

Before deployment, put each player's name in a hat, helmet or magical bag of some kind then, table by table, draw two names out at random to decide who is playing who on that table. The player whose name was drawn out first picks a table half and then deploys first, so you might want to draw one player for each table first so they can get on with setting up. Once you've done this for each of the battlefields do the same again to determine the foe.

The armies deploy in the same manner as for the Dawn Attack scenario (see Warhammer page 145).

Victory Conditions

Use victory points to determine the winner of each table.

The winners then go on to fight in a Battle Royale (see Warhammer page 406) on the centre table, using any surviving models – units regain D6 wounds, characters regain 1 Wound. The first player to finish his game deploys in the centre of the Morgheim battlefield, and each subsequent player may choose which board edge to deploy on. Play then proceeds as normal. The winner of the final battle is the player who has the most objectives.

MASS HYSTERIA!

The Marshes of Madness exert a strange influence on any who enter its mist-shrouded depths, causing soldiers to turn on their friends and driving men insane with horror.

At the start of each game fought in the Marshes of Madness roll a D6 for each unit. On a roll of a 1, the unit has succumbed to insanity. Roll again to see how the madness manifests:

1-2 **Gibbering Madness!** The unit is subject to Stupidity for the rest of the game as it plunges into insanity.

3-4 **Maddening Rage!** The unit is subject to Frenzy for the rest of the game as it is driven berserk by what it has seen.

5-6 **Inured to Insanity.** The unit gains the Immune to Psychology special rule for the rest of the game as it can see nothing worse than it has done already.

If at the start of the second game a 1 is rolled for a unit that went mad in the first game, do not roll to see what ails it. Instead it keeps the same insanity from the first game, and the effects are now permanent – mark them on the army roster.

ON DEADLY GROUND

There is little in the way of dry ground or safe paths in the Marshes of Madness, and you should try to use as much marshland terrain as possible – scattered flock or the base of a Citadel Wood can make for great marshes. Marshes are mysterious terrain – roll on the table on the right when a unit enters a marsh for the first time. In addition, other area terrain – forests, rivers, ruins and the like, but not buildings – count as Marshland in addition to their normal rules (although use their own mysterious table, if applicable).

1	Suffocating Swampland – An area of Khemrian Quicksand.
2	Septic Slough – Marshland with the rules of Necrotic Ooze.
3	Bubbling Bog – Marshland with the rules of a Boiling Flood.
4	Fumy Fen – A Mist-wreathed Swamp.
5	Macabre Morass – Marshland with the rules of a Charnel Pit.
6	Enchanted Everglade – An Earthblood Mere.

TO THE VICTORS THE SPOILS

Campaign Map Tile & Magic Items

The winner of each battle claims one of the Marshes of Madness tiles (including Morgheim). If there are more tiles than winners, then some of the players can win more than one. The winners also share the following magic items:

The Bog Standard
Magic Standard

This plain flag looks like little more than a rag on a stick.

One use only. The Bog Standard may be activated after charges have been declared but before distances have been rolled. Any enemy charging the unit this turn must make dangerous terrain tests as though charging through a marsh.

Fimir-skin Cloak
Talisman

The skin of a Fimir is gnarled, making it tough to work with. But to a dedicated artificer, a cloak fashioned from such a pelt is resistant to any blade.

The wearer of the cloak has a 6+ Scaly Skin save.

Mad Marsh Waders
Enchanted Item

These knee-high wading boots are waterproofed, allowing the wearer some small respite from the relentless damp.

The wearer of these magical boots and any unit he joins gain the Swamp Strider special rule, and are always steadfast when in a marsh.

The Crown of Nicodemos the Nonsensical
Enchanted Item

Once belonging to the deranged Hedge Wizard, Nicodemos, this modest crown was rumoured to be both the source of Nicodemos' power and his madness.

The wearer of this crown counts as a Level 1 Wizard, and knows a randomly generated spell from the Lore of Shadow (roll before each game). He also suffers from Stupidity.

Relics

Every player that takes part in the battle receives D3 relics, whether they win or lose their game.

DESCENT INTO MADNESS

Gaming Nights
One of the highlights of our campaign was the excuse to get together on gaming night, throw down the dice and let battle commence as challenges were fought and territory seized or lost. What the end of season games did was allow us to do this on a grand scale, so we'd not only gather en masse to game, but we'd gather to game *together*. Huge multiplayer battles are great fun, as are linked battles such as the ones played here. The sense of camaraderie that's gained as you see how your allies and enemies are faring is incomparable, and make for a great night of gaming!
Give it a try some time.

The end of season game for summer was a multi-table affair, with the winner of each battle going on to fight in a multi-player extravaganza. Six players gathered one evening – Andrew, Simon, Pete, Chris, Kevin and Tom – ready to fight it out for a piece of the Marshes of Madness and Morgheim itself.

Each of the boards was set up to resemble the Marshes of Madness: the first battlefield featured an overgrown road and mining camp; the second battlefield had a great tower rising from the middle; and the third table was covered in ruins.

Each player's name was put in a hat and a name drawn for each table. Chris ended up at the camp, Andrew at the tower and Simon at the ruin-strewn swamp. Each player set up in turn before their opponent was drawn, their army potentially spread out throughout their deployment zone.

Andrew found his army clustered in the centre of the board, with the exception of his Screaming Skull Catapult, Necrosphinx and Tomb Guard, who all started on the flanks. Pete found himself scattered across the board, with his Abomination on the

far flank (a whole table away from the Necrosphinx and Warsphinx, to both players' annoyance, as they wanted to see the huge monsters clash). Andrew's Tomb Guard succumbed to Stupidity, as did several of Pete's units.

Chris' army started out at the mining camp, his army packed tightly into the centre of his deployment zone (a little too tightly, Chris would freely admit, as his army was quite large and the central deployment area quite small). Many of his state troops succumbed to the madness, gaining Frenzy in the process. The Dwarfs were similarly addled, the maddening fumes from the swamp getting to the normally stoic warriors and driving them mad with rage. Rather appropriately, the Dwarfs found themselves clustered in the mining camp and the ruined watchtower.

Both the High Elves and the Warriors of Chaos managed to escape the worst of the madness, their proud leaders eyeing up the ruin-strewn battlefield with greedy eyes – whoever could tap into the power of the Arcane Ruins first would surely be able to unleash catastrophic magic upon the other.

GALBARAZ MINING CAMP

As the roving armies were overcome by the maddening mists of the marshes, even long-time friends and firm allies began to turn on one another. The Empire army led by Stiegfried Schweinsteiger himself stumbled upon an old abandoned mining camp near the edge of the swamps that Ravenbeard's Dwarfs were in the process of occupying. Succumbing to the effects of the marshes, the men saw not their allies but instead mistook them for bearded Goblins. Likewise the Dwarfs hallucinated a horde of skinny Orcs emerging from the undergrowth, and the two armies clashed. Both Chris and Kevin rolled 1s aplenty for their madness checks, a goodly chunk of their forces succumbing to Frenzy or Stupidity. The Dwarfs began the game hunkered down atop the hill in the lee of the ruined watchtower, whilst the Empire were clustered in front at the bottom. Despite their frenzied state troops, Chris' Empire struggled to shift the Dwarfs from the hill and despite an early victory achieved by downing Kevin's Gyrocopter, the battle looked bleak for the Empire. As the mist cleared, Schweinsteiger realised to his horror that they were no bearded Goblins at all but his sturdy Dwarf allies. He hoped that Karnji Ravenbeard would forgive him…

THE BLACK TOWER

Andrew wasted little time in getting started, knowing that he had to swiftly break the back of the Skaven horde before they could bring their superior numbers to bear. After some minor manoeuvring on both sides, Andrew launched his daring charges, his Tomb Guard rolling a double-6 and charging past the Abomination and into the unit of Clanrats beyond. Unfortunately the Tomb Kings' elite warriors could not scatter the Skaven fast enough, and the Tomb Guard found themselves locked in a brutal combat as the Abomination charged into their flank. Elsewhere the swamp-maddened Skavenslaves staggered forwards uncontrollably, bringing them before King Nekhenaten IV. The Tomb King charged forwards, smashing through the unit with ease but ending up right in front of the Hell Pit Abomination just as it finished chewing through the Tomb Guard. Although the Tomb King stepped forwards, Blade of Antarhak at hand, he could not stop the charge of the Abomination and his unit was soundly beaten. Pete was victorious, but despite his best efforts, he had failed to cast the Dreaded Thirteenth Spell and bolster his ranks for the final game with some transmuted reinforcements.

BITTERSAND SWAMP

Although the High Elves had set-up first, Tom managed to seize the initiative with a canny roll of a 6 and so took the first turn. The battlefield was saturated in magical energies bubbling up from the relics buried in the marsh, and so it was inevitable that a wizardly duel would occur. The High Elves unleashed a *Plague of Rust* upon the Chaos Warriors, causing their already tarnished armour to slough from their bodies as the blue iron decayed unnaturally. Far more devastatingly was the *Infernal Gateway* summoned by Acolyth Sextus, casting a proud regiment of Spearmen and a High Elf Mage into the Realm of Chaos! Simon responded by bolstering his Swordmasters with the power of the Lore of Life, but Tom wisely kept away from them until the spells had abated, charging in with Hellcannon, Chaos Knights and the Warshrine when it was safer to do so. Although the Elves put up a brave fight, they were eventually Thunderstomped into the mud and scattered before the Warriors of Chaos. The only ray of light for the High Elves was the downing of Ifrit Skybound by a hail of arrows, but as he eventually recovered, the Tomb Kings refused to make good on the bounty they had posted on him.

MORGHEIM

No blood was spared as the bitter rivals waded through the marshes to the ultimate prize – the ancient necropolis of Morgheim. After slaughtering their foes in the swamps beyond, the Dwarfs, Warriors of Chaos and Skaven prepared to do battle.

Having seen off the High Elves in short order, Tom's host of Chaos Warriors were the first to reach the ruined temple of Morgheim, and prepared to defend their find against any rival who sought to deny them their prize. It wasn't long before this caution proved wise, as Kevin's Dwarfs arrived from the west shortly afterwards, followed moments later by the Pete's Skaven, who scuttled onto the battlefield from the north.

Battle was joined in earnest, with the Skaven surging towards the temple and wiping out Tom's Chaos Ogres with overwhelming numbers. Safe in the knowledge that it would be some time before Kevin's Dwarf host could challenge any of his objectives, Tom concentrated his efforts on driving the Skaven back. After a protracted combat, the Chaos Knights cut down Pete's Hell Pit Abomination, though not before losing most of their number to the beast's fearsome attacks. Tom's Chaos Warriors drove the Skaven before them, but Pete soon changed tact and transformed a full unit of 18 Chaos Warriors into Clanrats!

Having spent the first half of the battle slowly advancing towards the action, Kevin's Hammerer's finally made their presence felt, smashing through a unit of Chaos Warriors and arriving at the central objective. But their moment of triumph was short-lived, as Pete's Grey Seer turned all 22 of the survivors into Clanrats and ultimately forced a draw! With Tom defeated, Kevin and Pete shared the honours.

Ka-blam!
As the game drew to an end, Kevin's Dwarfs were in control of two objectives, whilst Pete was only in control of one. On the final turn Pete launched his cunning plan, charging the Dwarf Warriors with his Clanrats, ensuring that neither side controlled the objective, and then casting Skitterleap on his Warlock Engineer to capture Kev's second objective. However, he had not counted on the accuracy of the Dwarf gunners, as they unleashed a storm of shot at the Skaven Wizard, blowing him to smithereens. The game ended in a draw.

The Horned Rat Sends his Regards

Although Pete had failed at his goal to enter Morgheim with more models than he'd had in his army at the start of the evening's gaming, it didn't take him long to make some new friends in the deathly city. His Grey Seer wasted no time in casting the Dreaded Thirteenth Spell on both the Chaos Warriors and the Dwarf Hammerers, adding another 40 Clanrats to his army!

Annotations

A Kevin's army is too far away to engage in the early stages of the battle, but the Dwarf artillery nonetheless reaps a fearsome toll on their enemies.

B Augmented by *Death Frenzy*, Pete's Stormvermin carve apart the Chaos Ogres in the blink of an eye.

C Having regenerated an extraordinary number of wounds, the Hell Pit Abomination finally succumbs to the relentless attacks of the Chaos Knights.

D The Hammers utilise their Devastating Charge veteran ability to annihilate the Chaos Warriors in a single brutal round of combat…

E …Before being turned into Clanrats and inadvertently claiming the central objective for the sneaky Skaven!

BLOOD IN THE BADLANDS
AUTUMN

AUTUMN CAMPAIGN TURN

Annotations

A The winners of the end of summer game divide the Marshes of Madness – and Morgheim – between them.

B Although Simon's High Elves reclaim much of their empire from the Skaven, Andy's Raiding Party steal another territory.

C Kevin's Sappers send one of Andy's castles tumbling to the ground – probably not the greatest of accomplishments, given their ramshackle nature.

D Andrew and Pete fight a Storm of Magic battle, the Tomb Kings beating the Skaven at their own game.

E The Skaven of Clan Mange lay siege to the Dwarfen outer fortress of Dok Karaz, hauling their experimental Warp-Magma Doom Cannon to battle. Predictably, it detonates spectacularly.

F Tom feeds Andrew's army Bad Intelligence, moving a Tomb Kings army into a trap laid by his Chaos Warriors.

G The Warriors of Chaos defeat King Nekhenaten IV in battle and capture his mummified form.

H Despite the Red Witch's valiant rescue attempt, Mawrhin Skell consumes the essence of King Nekhenaten IV.

A Tangled Web

At the start of the campaign, each of the players had to nominate one player to be their ally. This created a tangled web that could roughly be divided into two factions. Both Chris and Andrew were firmly allied to Kevin's Dwarfs, and although Simon's High Elves were contemptuous of all the other forces a truce held between them and the Dwarfs of Barak Varr. On the other side, things were less clear cut. Both Skaven players presented a united front, although they were constantly seeking to outdo one another behind the scenes. Tom and Matt were nominally allied with them, although Tom changed his allies at random and Matt had tricked the forces of the Empire into thinking they were really the Counts of Stirland.

As Fozzrik's Flying Fastness made its penultimate swoop of the Badlands, the fledgeling empires attempted a desperate grab for land. Whoever held the largest realm had the best chance gaining ingress to the ensorcelled fortress.

Seasonal Rule

For two seasons the Flying Fastness has flown across the Badlands. In its wake, a magical storm has roiled and lashed out across the land.

Any Storm of Magic games played during Autumn grants both players a relic. Any Storm of Magic games played in a tile adjacent to the Flying Fastness grant 2 relics instead of 1.

With summer over, darker skies spread across the Badlands, and with it, darker tidings. The forces of Morivar Darkstalker, dread Vampire Lord took full advantage of the longer nights and set out on an unprecedented land grab. Expeditions of the Undead spearheaded northwards, taking realm after realm from empires that had turned their attention elsewhere. But with Darkstalker unable to leave any meaningful force behind to guard these new lands (there were no nearby populations to turn into Zombies), it would surely only be a matter of time before they are retaken once the defending armies return in force.

In the west, the colony of Prince Aurelian of Yvresse had been struggling with a pest problem since the beginning of summer. Sent by the Screaming One, ratmen invaded through the mines and have been taking land from Prince's Aurelian's empire ever since. However, autumn proved to be the Skaven's undoing. As always, they had over-extended themselves fighting against not just the Empire in the centre of the Badlands but also attacking Barak Varr from above and below. With the Vermin Lord's attention elsewhere, Aurelian's forces made a determined effort to push back the Skaven and vanquish

them from the coast of the Black Gulf once and for all. The High Elves were partially successful, banishing the ratmen from the Ivory Tower and nearby mineworks, but still the Skaven clung to a few rocky outcrops of land, much to the Prince's frustration. This meant that come the winter, Aurelian would still have to commit forces to wiping out the infernal Skaven invasion, rather than expanding his own empire.

Meanwhile, the Chaos Sorcerer, Ifrit Skybound, had managed to capture the Tomb King, Nekhenaten IV, once more. It was actually a comet called down by the Sorcerer that did the damage. The comet crashed from the sky and scored a direct hit that pulverised the Tomb King, allowing Ifrit Skybound to collect the powdered form of the fearsome Tomb King.

A rescue attempt was made by the Red Witch to retrieve her liege with an army of Ushabti, but was too late. Skybound's master, Mawrhin Skell, distilled the Tomb King's essence into an elixir and imbibed him before the Ushabti could cut through the defending Chosen.

Back at Barak Varr, the Skaven of Clan Mange attempted a full frontal siege of Dok Karaz, unveiling their insidious doomsday machine, the Warp-Magma Doom Cannon, but it exploded in spectacular fashion…

Amidst the Storm

In a cunning attempt to double up on relics, Andrew and Pete played a Storm of Magic game. Andrew, who, of course, was now without his original Tomb King set about flattening the 'other' Skaven, those of a certain Mr Foley.

The Skaven started well, aggressively advancing and keen to get to grips with the skeletal hordes. However, Pete didn't count on Andrew being able to cast *Return of the Golden Age,* thereby augmenting the entire Tomb King army. Fortune continued to smile on the boney ones as Andrew made two spectacular charges, one involved his Necrosphinx, which swooped across the table to slice Pete's Grey Seer in two, and the other saw his Tomb Guard move a maximum of 16" to bypass the Hell Pit Abomination and charge into a pack of surprised Stormvermin. Needless to say, the Tomb Kings won the day and the Skaven racked up another loss.

King Neher, the first of his name, is henceforth declared inheritor of the golden throne of Naqqara, and as his first action declares unending vengeance upon Mawrhin Skell. Any who bring him the head of this betentacled warrior will be granted first pick from the loot!

My silence conveys my contempt – The Emberblade, Lord Skell

– Tom and Andrew air their views on the Tomb King's death via email.

Pest Control Required

Dear Allies,

It pains me to ask, but if anyone could spare some of their military might to help an old and loyal friend in his quest to rid his modest empire of these horrid little beasts, then I would be forever grateful and in your debt.

Yours,
Prince Aurelian

Warp-Doom-Magma

Losing patience with the underground campaign, and feeling, perhaps, overly-confident due to successes elsewhere on the map, Andy attempted to take Dok Karaz, in an all-out assault. Andy wasn't totally naive to think he could breach a Dwarf Fortress on his own. For he had secured a secret weapon, by seconding Chris Peach's rather wonderful Warp-Magma Doom Cannon. A thing of insane beauty, all it needed was some equally insane rules, which both Andy and Kev came up with (you can see these on page 93).

Unfortunately, as is the law with Skaven experimental weaponry, a misfire result should be appropriately bad, and this is what Andy rolled on the first turn of the game. So rather than blowing a hole in Kev's fortress walls the doomsday weapon blew up itself! Deprived of his secret weapon, Andy nevertheless tried to continue his siege, but the Dwarfs' own artillery proved to be far more sturdy and sent the Skaven scuttling away with tails between their legs.

AUTUMN SCENARIO
GEHEIMNISNACHT

The Night of Mysteries. Winter's Eve. Ar'Uzkul. Twilight's Tide. Call it what you will, but the night when Morrslieb hangs full in the sky can only bring ill will and more blood to the war-torn Badlands.

The denizens of the Warhammer world know all too well that strange things happen on Geheimnisnacht. In the Badlands, it is said that an eerie ethereal tower appears, and from it radiates a swirling arcane vortex. This tower is known by a few as the 'Gatehouse' although the providence of that title has only now been revealed with the Flying Fastness soaring in the skies above. The Gatehouse is the tether – an anchor point that will allow the Flying Fastness to come to rest upon the ground once more. Whoever has control of the Gatehouse when it appears on Winter's Eve will have a powerful advantage when it comes to breaching the Flying Fastness next season.

The Armies

This scenario is for two evenly matched teams. Each player chooses his force using the list from a Warhammer Armies book, to an equal points value agreed before the game. In addition each player can spend an extra 25% of the value again on Scrolls of Binding, Pacts and Mythic Artefacts. They may also include one lieutenant for free, if they are a Wizard or Runesmith and cost no more than 500 points.

The Battlefield

Set up the battlefield as described in Storm of Magic, allowing roughly 2' x 2' per player. Do not place Arcane Fulcrums yet, but place a large terrain piece in the centre, such as Skullvane Manse, Lair of the Astromancer. Each player then takes a single Arcane Fulcrum. Roll off to see which player places the first one – they pick a 2' x 2' section and deploy their fulcrum in the centre point of it.

Deployment

After they have deployed their Arcane Fulcrum, each player must place a Wizard (or Runesmith or Runelord) on top of it.

Once each player has done this, roll-off once more to determine the order of deployment. Each player may deploy his units within 12" of his table edge or within 6" of their Arcane Fulcrum. Any units that cannot be deployed enter play following the rules for reinforcements, arriving during the first turn.

First Turn

Once all of the players have deployed individually, each team rolls off to see who has the first turn. The game then proceeds as normal, with each team taking a turn.

Game Length

The game will last for six turns, or until a time limit agreed by the players is reached, whichever comes first.

Victory Conditions

At the end of the game, whichever team controls the most Arcane Fulcrums wins the battle. If both teams control the same number, the team that controls Fozzrik's Gatehouse wins. If neither team controls the Gatehouse, use Victory Points to break the tie.

FOZZRIK'S GATEHOUSE

Fozzrik's Gatehouse:
The gateway to Fozzrik's Flying Fastness only opens when Morrslieb is full and a storm of magic howls strong, manifesting itself as an Arcane Fulcrum that only a powerful Mage can hope to harness. To represent this in the game, Fozzrik's Gatehouse counts as both an Arcane Fulcrum and a Mysterious Wizard's Tower (see page 76 of Storm of Magic).

Scenario Special Rules:
In addition to the rules for Fozzrik's Gatehouse described above, this game uses the following scenario special rules, the details for which can all be found in Storm of Magic:

Magical Flux, Arcane Fulcrums, Wild Magic, Cantrips and Cataclysm spells.

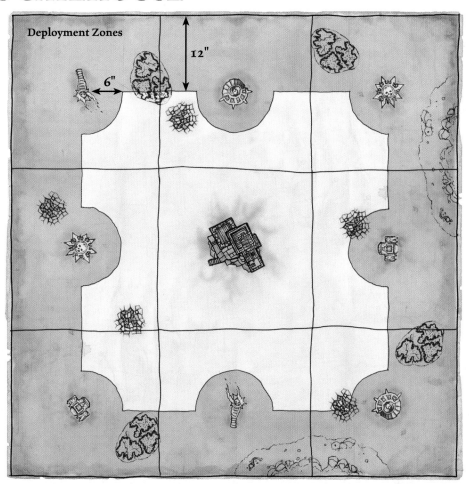

Deployment Zones

12"

6"

TO THE VICTORS THE SPOILS

Every player (winner or loser) gains D3 relics. If a player ends the game in control of an Arcane Fulcrum, they gain D6 relics instead. The players on the winning side must then share out the following magic items:

The Tetragon of Tectonic Displacement
Arcane Item
An artefact whose origins lie in the distant past, when the configuration of the tetragon is altered the very earth surrounding the user shifts.

Bound Spell (Power level 10). One Use Only. The Tetragon of Tectonic Displacement contains the *Ribauld's Retroactive Illusion* spell (Lore of Shadows).

Helm of the Headless Horseman
Magic Armour
To wear the Helm of the Headless Horseman is to tempt fate, for it is said that when Morrslieb waxes full the Headless Horseman comes to take his helmet back…

The wearer counts his armour save as being one higher than normal. The wearer's close combat attacks have both the Killing Blow and Flaming Attacks special rules.

Banner of the Valkyrie
Magic Standard
The Banner of the Valkyrie flutters violently as though in a storm, even when the winds are calm.

One Use Only. Until the start of the next player turn, the unit carrying this standard gains the Fly special rule.

The Shard of Morrslieb
Talisman
This necklace bears a shard fallen from the moon of Morrslieb, a baleful talisman that fills the wearer with a deathless vigour.

The bearer is immune to Killing Blow and Poisoned Attacks, which must roll to wound as normal. He is also immune to the effects of spells from the Lore of Death.

Claiming Fozzrik's Gatehouse
The player who controls Fozzrik's Gatehouse at the end of the game (regardless of whether or not his team won) may place it in any non-capital tile in his empire. For the rest of the campaign, that territory is worth an additional five relics to the controlling player.

RACE FOR THE GATEHOUSE

With the campaign about to enter its final quarter, alliances are tested and friendships strained as everyone races to the Gatehouse hoping to be the first to claim the secrets and rewards held within.

An unholy alliance had formed between the Screaming One, Chaos Lord Mawhrin Skel and dread Vampire Morivar Darkstalker. Three of the most evil and insidious creatures striding the mortal planes were opposed by the Red Witch – seeking vengeance for the permanent death of her liege – Archmage Hothar the Fey, Dwarf Lord Karnji and the irrepressible Empire General, Schweinsteiger. The second Skaven contingent was noticeably absent despite reassurances of their presence – was treachery abound?

The three lords of Destruction agreed that the gatehouse needed to be under their sway from the first turn, as this would give them Dominance, and access to the most powerful Cataclysm spells. It would also compel the forces of Order to advance. But just as the Chaos and Undead were agreeing that it should be Tom's Daemon Prince to take the Gatehouse, Andy measured the distance and immediately placed his Vermin Lord inside, claiming it for the Skaven – the sneaky swine!

Despite the chuntering from the Forces of Destruction players, the rest of the Skaven, Chaos and Undead units advanced, guarding the fulcrums, their magic users had deployed on as well as moving within charge range of the enemy.

Having captured the Gatehouse so early the Forces of Destruction had Dominance from the very start and so had a whole new level of Cataclysm spells to use…

Dominance

Between them, the three Destruction players had access to over 40 spells, and gleefully set about deciding what evil conjuration to cast on the foes first. Andy stepped forward to cast *Verminous Ruin,* a vortex that could well leave another Vermin Lord in its wake. This was wisely dispelled by the High Elves (no doubt Tom and Matt were pleased the spell was stopped as well).

A The Forces of Destruction claim the first turn, but as Tom and Matt discuss which of their Wizards should claim Fozzrik's Gatehouse, Andy sneakily seizes it with his Vermin Lord whilst his 'allies' are distracted!

B The Screaming One successfully calls down the Dreaded Thirteenth Spell on Simon's unit of Swordmasters, but miscasts in the attempt. The Vermin Lord escapes unscathed, but the wild magical discharge forms a magical eclipse which shrouds the entire battlefield.

C As the deadly magic begins to take hold on the Swordmasters, the fell magic is drained harmlessly away by the Battle Standard Bearer's Banner of the World Dragon.

D Kevin hammers the Dragon Ogre Shaggoth and Hell Pit Abomination with cannon fire, inflicting grievous injuries on both of the monsters.

E Simon's Hydra cuts down Tom's Chaos Sorcerer hiding in the woods with its venomous spit.

F Chris' bound Giant rampages into the Bloodcrushers, roaring so loud it slays two Daemons!

G The Dwarfs and Chaos Warriors fight each other to a bloody stalemate.

H After a multitude of Thundercrush and Thunderstomp attacks, Andrew's Khemrian Warsphinx tramples over the last few Bloodletters.

Bad Manners

With the onset of a Magical Eclipse courtesy of the Vermin Lord's miscast spell, the battlefield had become shrouded in an unnatural darkness, reducing all charge, spell and shooting ranges to a paltry 14". Tom justifiably believed that his lone Chaos Sorcerer was safe from the Hydra prowling nearby. What he didn't realise was that Simon had upgraded his Hydra with Spit Venom, and promptly unleashed his pet's toxic discharge, slaying Tom's wizard.

A MAELSTROM OF MELEES

Tipping the Balance

In many close combat situations, finding a way to change your required dice rolls even by a single point is often all that is needed to tip the odds of winning the fight your favour. This is where Hex and Augment spells come in.

Having charged his White Lions into Tom's second unit of Chaos Warriors to protect the flank of Kevin's Dwarf Warriors, Simon was able to give his unit the edge with a single Hex spell. By casting *Transmutation of Lead*, the Strength 6 High Elves would now only need a 3+ to hit the Chaos Warriors, with (re-rolls for their Speed of Asuryan special rule), and strip them of their modified 6+ armour save.

If the first turn had been a strong one for the Forces of Destruction, the second turn left a lot to be desired. All charges, of which there was no less that five, failed, and so the Shaggoth failed to contact the Runesmith upon the Arcane Fulcrum, the Stonehorn and Giant Spined Chaos Beast failed their charge and even the Hell Pit Abomination just blundered about in the southwest. The Magic Phase was no better, with the Vermin Lord failing to cast the Dreaded Thirteenth Spell despite rolling six dice. The Forces of Order were far more successful with the Khemrian Warsphinx smashing into the Bloodletters and the Giant bound by the Empire hitting the Bloodcrushers. The Giant surprised everyone by winning the combat – in fact his yell and bawling caused two of the Bloodcrushers to de-stabilise, sucking them back to the Realm of Chaos. They were obviously not up for a fight – strange considering their patron god is Khorne!

The third turn saw the armies really get to grip, with each other. Along the east flank, the monsters belonging to Tom and Matt started to strike home, the Great Spined Beast proved especially effective,

by slaying the Red Witch atop her Arcane Fulcrum. In retaliation, the Warsphinx rose up on its hind legs and smashed down on the Bloodletters – who would have been well and truly pulped if they hadn't been made of magic!

Across to the west the High Elves and Dwarfs were tackling the twin-threats of Chaos Warriors and Skaven. The Chaos Warriors were closer and so took the brunt of the Dwarfs' and White Lions' counter charges. The Dwarfs were eventually cut down, but the second unit of Chaos Warriors that faced the White Lions could not hold against the savage onslaught of the High Elves. The White Lions overran into the Chaos War Shrine and were promptly charged in the side by 40 Clanrats.

The Forces of Destruction now had two Arcane Fulcrums more than their foes, but the Order players were not ready to give up just yet. Tom's Tzeentchi Sorcerer was shot off his fulcrum in a hail of Tomb King archery. And in a rather unlucky chain of events, Kev's Dwarf Cannon blew the Vermin Lord apart. This allowed Chris' Battle Wizard to nip in and take the Gatehouse on the final turn of the battle.

An Abominable Presence

The Hell Pit Abomination had spent the first half of the battle limping about, achieving very little, and getting shot at by flaming cannonballs. But the appearance of the Pistoliers from the north finally gave the Abomination something to literally get its various sets of teeth into. However, the sight of such a disgusting and monstrous creature bearing down on them was too much for the Pistoliers who turned tail and fled before it could reach them. This had the unfortunate consequence for the High Elf Spearmen standing just behind – they would make an ideal replacement meal and so were hit in the flank. The High Elves put up a spirited defence but could not stand before the rampaging monster that smashed amongst them in an avalanche of flesh. The High Elves fled effectively collapsing the north west flank and leaving Kev's Dwarfs unsupported, their only allies were the White Lions who were busy slaughtering the horde of Skaven Clanrats in their flank.

The next meal in line for the Abomination was a Battle Wizard, looking very lonely on his Arcane Fulcrum. Luckily, there were a few spare Arcane Fulcrums about to jump to – all he had to do now was get his teleport spell off…

A Froggy Disposition

In the closing moments of the battle, Chris' wizard miscast and turned all the magic users into Frogs. The Warsphinx had charged Tom's Daemon Prince and all it had to do was slay it to draw the game. You would have thought that a Warsphinx matched against a frog would be a foregone conclusion, but that 3+ Ward Save kept Tom in it, and meant that the game ended in a win for Tom, Andy and Matt!

King of the Castle

The Screaming One had held the Gatehouse since the first turn of the game, but all that was about to change. Kev fired his Dwarf Cannon at the Gatehouse, and caused 5 hits (you roll a D6, just like for any template weapon). All wounded but Andy was unfazed, after all he had a 3+ Ward Save... which he promptly failed, on all five dice. The Vermin Lord was utterly destroyed and the Gatehouse was up for grabs again.

Chris Peach took full advantage and moved his Battle Wizard into the vacant Gatehouse. The Forces of Destruction were able to claim victory by being in control of four Arcane Fulcrums to the three occupied by the forces of Order, but it was Sweinsteiger's Empire that held the Gatehouse at the end of the day, and so claimed the gatehouse. All of a sudden the Empire were in a strong position as thoughts turned to winter, and the final phase of the campaign.

As for the Screaming One – when asked if he would make a reappearance in the campaign, Andy was quite blunt on the matter: 'No, he's very dead!'. Clan Mange would continue without their Daemonic Overlord.

UNDERGROUND BATTLES

Optional Rule

As the armies fight, the raucous battle shakes the very walls and ceiling of the cavern – beware of falling Stalactites!

To add even more peril to your underground games why not try these optional rules.

At the start of every player turn, the player whose turn it is rolls a D3. This is how many stalactites have fallen from the cave ceiling. Starting with that player, take the small template and place it anywhere on the battlefield and then scatter 2D6". Anything under the template when it comes to rest must take a Strength 4 hit, normal saves apply. If a 'hit' is rolled, the template still scatters, but only by the amount of the lowest D6. The opposing player then places the next stalactite in the same manner, and if there is a third, the first player gets to place it.

Whilst the battle rages across the surface of the Old World the nefarious Skaven have taken a new tack in the war for Fozzrik's Flying Fastness. By undermining the citadel of Barak Varr they aim to steal the knowledge of the Dwarfs, while incidentally removing one of their main competitors. The ratmen have undoubtedly come up with a cunning plan that should give them an unprecedented advantage in this quest for ultimate power. With only the stalwart Dwarfs to prevent their wicked schemes it is surely only a matter of time before the Council of Thirteen are celebrating another step towards their inevitable domination of the world!

To represent this new turn in the campaign we created a special underground section of the Mighty Empires campaign map. In addition to the normal campaign turn and resulting battles Pete or Andy's Skaven may challenge Kevin to a game in the tunnels below the Old World. Should Pete or Andy be victorious they may move their campaign marker along one step towards Kevin's capital. If Kevin wins the Skaven advance is halted and they must replay the scenario the next time they meet. Should both Andy and Pete decided to challenge Kev then they must both play together using the rules for Fragile alliances as described in the Warhammer rulebook.

The special rules for these underground games are detailed below:

Battles Below The Earth

Irrepressible Gloom: The range of all shooting attacks and spells is limited to 24", and all attacks beyond 6" count as being at long range.

Uncertain Footing & Low Ceilings: Cavalry, monstrous cavalry and all flyers must take a Dangerous Terrain test whenever they make a march, charge, flee or pursue move.

Trolls & Cave Squigs: The deep places of the Warhammer world are infested with Trolls and Cave Squigs. To represent this, after setting up terrain but before deployment, roll to see how many of these creatures have made their lairs on the battlefield. On the roll of a 4+, there are D3 Trolls present, regardless of the outcome, there are always D6 Cave Squigs. The players take it in turn to set up these neutral models anywhere on the battlefield, but at least 6" away from each other and either side's deployment zone. These models will move D6" in a random direction in each player's Compulsory Moves phase, fighting anyone they come into contact with, but never pursuing. They are treated as enemy models to both sides. See Warhammer: Orcs & Goblins for rules and profiles.

SECURE A PAWHOLD

The chittering and scrabbling of a thousand paws announces the arrival of the Skaven. The Dwarfs are caught unawares but they have the Skaven in a bottleneck as they emerge into the cavernous halls of the Dwarven realm. Can they hold them at the gates and prevent the verminous hordes from gaining a foothold?

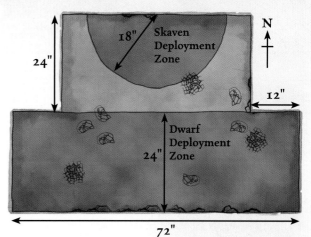

The Armies
The Dwarf player may choose an army of up to 1000 points from Warhammer Armies: Dwarfs. The Skaven player may choose an army of up to 1500 points from Warhammer Armies: Skaven.

The Battlefield
Set up the battlefield as shown on the map, using terrain such as rocky outcrops and pillars instead of using the Random Terrain chart.

Deployment
The Dwarf army deploys first, anywhere within 24" of the long table side. The Skaven player then deploys his army within 18" of the short table edge's centre point (see map).

First Turn
As the Skaven have taken the Dwarfs by surprise, they have the first turn.

Game Length
The game will last for six game turns, or until a time limit agreed by the players is reached, whichever comes first.

Victory Conditions
The Skaven are trying to break the Dwarf army as quickly as possible in order to gain a foothold in the Dwarfen Realms. The Skaven player wins if the Dwarf army has lost all of its standards or, by the time the game ends, there are six or more unbroken Skaven units (excluding characters or war machines) within the Dwarf player's deployment zone. If neither of these situations has been met by the time the game ends, then the Dwarf player wins.

POISON THE WELLS

The nefarious Skaven have targeted fresh water wells that supply the hold. Calling in the expert services of Clan Eshin, the ingenious Warlords see an opportunity to deny the Dwarfs this precious resource.

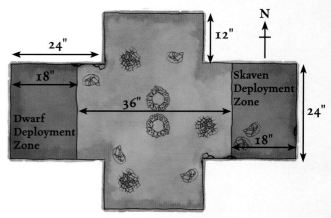

The Armies
The Dwarf player may choose an army of up to 1500 points from Warhammer Armies: Dwarfs. The Skaven player may choose an army of up to 1500 points from Warhammer Armies: Skaven, but must include at least one Clan Eshin Assassin, who will deploy hidden in a friendly unit as usual.

The Battlefield
Set up the battlefield as shown on the map, using terrain such as rocky outcrops and pillars. In the centre of the board there are two deep pools of water – these are the wells of Barak Varr that the Skaven are attempting to poison.

Deployment
Players take it in turn to place units on the table, using the alternating units method of deployment described on page 142 of Warhammer. See the map for deployment zones.

First Turn
Roll off to see which player takes the first turn. The player that finished deploying his army first adds +1 to his roll.

Game Length
The game will last for six game turns, or until the Skaven player has poisoned the both wells (see below).

Victory Conditions
The Skaven player may attempt to poison one of the wells if one of his units with a revealed Skaven Assassin is in base contact with it at the start of his turn. The Skaven player must roll a dice. If he scores a 3 or more, he has poisoned the well. However, if the Assassin, or the unit he has joined, is in close combat, then he receives a -2 penalty to this roll. If, at the end of Turn 6, the Skaven have poisoned one of the wells, they achieve a minor victory and may move on to the next space on the map. If the Skaven poison both wells, the game ends immediately with a major Skaven victory. Should this occur, the Dwarf forces will struggle to resupply and will suffer 100 points penalty in every underground battle for the remainder of the campaign.

The Dwarfs barricade the underground passage, but the Skaven are determined to pass.

UNDERMINE THE DEFENCES SCENARIO THREE

The defences of Barak Varr are nigh impregnable to an attack on the surface. The Skaven have no intention of doing so without first weakening the impenetrable fortifications from below...

The Armies

The Dwarf player may choose an army of up to 1500 points. The Skaven player may choose an army of up to 1500 points.

The Battlefield

Set up the battlefield as shown on the map with rocky outcrops and pillars. In the centre of each of the four central board sections stands a mighty pillar, a so-called Earthstone.

Deployment

Players take it in turn to place units on the table, using the alternating units method of deployment described on page 142 of Warhammer. See the map for deployment zones. The Dwarf player places first.

First Turn

Roll off to see which player takes the first turn. The player that finished deploying his army first adds +1 to his roll.

Game Length

The game will last for six game turns, or until the Skaven player has destroyed the Earthstones (see below).

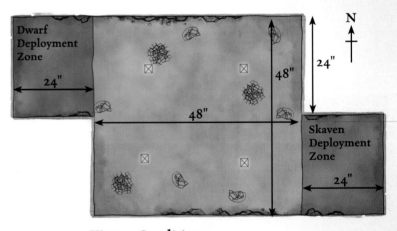

Victory Conditions

The Skaven are attempting to destroy the Earthstones. The Earthstones are treated as buildings that cannot be occupied, with a Toughness of 10 and 5 Wounds each. Skaven units in base contact with an Earthstone may direct their close combat attacks against, hitting automatically. If, at the end of Turn 6, the Skaven have destroyed three Earthstones, they achieve a minor victory and may move on to the next space of the map. If the Skaven destroy all four, the game ends with a major Skaven victory. Should this occur, the surface defences will be irreparably damaged by the collapsed Earthstones, and the Dwarf player will lose his racial map bonus for the remainder of the campaign.

CLAIM THE APPROACH

Having made steady progress towards Barak Varr, the Skaven seek to secure a narrow approach that leads to the underground gateway of the Dwarf hold. Can the Dwarfs finally stymie the advance of the rat-men here?

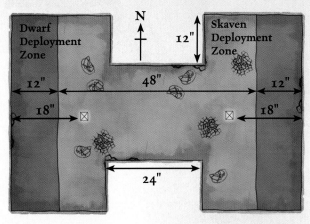

The Armies

The Dwarf player may choose an army of up to 2000 points, but must also prepare a 500-point reserve force. The Skaven player may choose an army of up to 2000 points.

The Battlefield

Set up the battlefield as shown on the map, using terrain such as rocky outcrops and pillars. There are two objectives, marked by Dwarf Runestones.

Deployment

Players take it in turn to place units on the table, using the alternating units method of deployment described on page 142 of Warhammer. See the map for deployment zones. The Dwarf player places the first. The Dwarf reserve force arrives from the eastern table edge on Turn 3, using the rules for reinforcements on page 27 of Warhammer.

First Turn

Roll off to see which player takes the first turn. The player that finished deploying his army first adds +1 to his roll.

Game Length

The game will last for six game turns, or until a time limit agreed by the players is reached, whichever comes first.

Victory Conditions

The Skaven are after the two Runestones that control vast gateways either side of the narrow approach. If, at the end of Turn 6, the Skaven have secured the western Runestone, they achieve a minor victory and may move on to the next space on the map. If the Skaven secure both Runestones, they earn an additional 500 points to field in Scenario 5.

STORMING THE GATES OF BARAK VARR

The Skaven have overrun the underground defences of the Dwarfs and made their way to the very gates of Barak Varr itself. Only the legendary courage and tenacity of the Dwarfs can save them now.

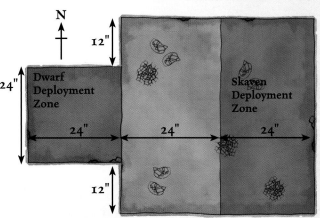

The Armies

The Dwarf player may choose an army of up to 2500 points. In addition, as this is the last defence of their Hold, the entire Dwarf army gains the Stubborn special rule. The Skaven player may choose an army of up to 2500 points.

The Battlefield

Set up the battlefield as shown on the map, using terrain such as rocky outcrops and pillars instead of using the Random Terrain Chart.

Deployment

The Dwarf player deploys his entire army first, anywhere on the western board section. The Skaven player then deploys his units anywhere within 24" of the eastern table edge.

First Turn

After deployment, the Dwarf player rolls a dice. On a roll of a 6, he can choose who has the first turn. On a roll of 1-5, the Skaven player chooses who has the first turn.

Game Length

The game will last for six game turns, or until a time limit agreed by the players is reached, whichever comes first.

Victory Conditions

The Skaven are attempting to breach the gateway to Barak Varr behind the Dwarf lines. If, at the end of Turn 6, three or more unbroken Skaven units (excluding characters or war machines) escaped off the western table edge, the Skaven player wins. Any other result ends in a Dwarf victory. If the Skaven win this scenario, the Dwarf capital is invaded from below and the Dwarf player permanently loses one campaign army, which is forced withdraw and defend the underground breach. In addition, the Dwarf capital counts as a permanent mine resource for every Skaven player, which never collapses or runs dry. All Skaven players also gain D6+3 relics each, as they raid the hold's treasury.

THE WAR FOR BARAK VARR

United by the common cause of infiltrating and destroying the Dwarf Hold of Barak Varr, the Skaven Clans Mange and Mors begun their subterranean assault on its unwitting defenders.

From the Pits of Hell

Pete's Hell Pit Abomination was to prove a nigh-unstoppable menace to Kevin's forces throughout the War for Barak Varr. In standard battles, Kevin claims to have little trouble dealing with big, regenerating monsters, as he always upgrades his Cannons with the Rune of Fire, robbing them of their natural protection.

However, the Irrepressible Gloom special rule that applied to the underground battles really hampered the effectiveness of Kevin's artillery, and he paid for this handicap with many Dwarf lives. This problem was also exacerbated by Pete's outrageous fortune when it came to passing his 4+ regenerate saves against non-Flaming Attacks! Pete's Abomination now features many times in Kevin's Book of Grudges.

The Skaven infiltration of the Dwarf Underway surrounding Barak Varr began late on in the spring season. Up until this point, both of the Skaven warlords had been focusing their efforts on grabbing as much land as possible in the opening turns of the campaign. However, with the eight warring armies having staked their claim to much of the available territory in the Badlands, Andy and Pete began to turn their attentions elsewhere.

So it was that week four saw the Skaven take their first anxious steps into the Dwarf realm. Not wanting to waste their inaugural opportunity to make inroads into Kevin's subterranean territory, both Andy and Pete joined forces to lend their combined experience (OK, mainly Pete's!) to the task.

Combining their wisdom and resources proved to be a wise decision for the Skaven generals. Selecting their additional 500 points with utmost ruthlessness, Andy and Pete overwhelmed Kevin's thin Dwarf line, wiping them out to the last beardling. Kevin had elected to theme his army on a Dwarf scouting party that had encountered the Skaven vanguard as they poured through the breach and into the Underway beneath Barak Varr. Leaving their war machines back at the hold, the Dwarf army consisted primarily of two large units of Rangers and a supporting regiment of Crossbowmen. Sadly for the valiant defenders, they proved

no match for the pair of Doomwheels and the swarming hordes of Clanrats that faced them, and the Dwarfs fell beneath the weight of numbers and humming bolts of warp lightning.

Kevin's luck failed to improve as the summer season kicked off on the surface. Having established an underground foothold, Pete decided to try his luck at the second scenario and push the Skaven assault deeper into the Underway. Despite the legendary tenacity of the Dwarfs, Kevin's brave warriors were unable to bring down Pete's Hell Pit Abomination until turn 6. During that time, the abhorrent creature had torn the majority of the small Dwarf host to pieces, and a hapless Kevin could do little to stop the clandestine work of the Skaven Assassin. The Clan Eshin agent successfully poisoned both wells, costing Kevin a 100 point penalty to his army list in any further battles underground.

The Dwarfs were to prove too much for Andy's Skaven as they tried to bring down the mighty Earthstone pillars in Scenario 3. The Skaven poured forth into the Dwarf halls, but only managed to destroy a single column before they were driven from the battlefield by a determined defence. The onset of autumn saw Clan Fawsquikk try where Clan Mange had failed, but Pete was also thwarted by Kevin's disciplined defence of his homeland.

On the third attempt at scenario 3, the Skaven generals combined their forces once more to challenge Kevin's realm. Despite Kevin slaying Pete's seemingly blessed (or should that be cursed?) Hell Pit Abomination with his first shot as soon as it came into range of his Cannon, the relentless waves of Skaven attacks were just enough to bring down three Earthstones and secure passage to the next campaign tile. However, the blow of losing more ground to the Skaven advance was somewhat lessened for Kevin by the fact that his surface defences would remain unaffected, as he had suffered only a minor defeat in this scenario.

The Skaven of Clan Mange returned in week four of autumn to secure the approach to Barak Varr itself. In an entirely thematic display of 'hammer & anvil' tactics, Kevin smashed Andy's first attempt to overrun his position and claim the objective he needed to secure victory. However, Andy is notoriously stubborn and it wasn't long before he launched another determined attack on Kevin's realm.

So it was that mid-winter saw Clan Mange on the warpath once again. Andy had obviously learnt from his mistakes, as this time Kevin's forces were taken completely by storm. Led by a Hell Pit Abomination, a Doomwheel and supported by the fell magic of a Grey

Seer, Andy's furious attack on Kevin's battleline caused so much damage that he was able to bring a large portion of his vastly superior numbers to bear on Kevin's reinforcements, crushing them in short order. The ramifications of this victory were serious indeed – the Skaven forces would now be bolstered by a further 500 points when it came to their final attack on the underground entrance to Barak Varr.

The Skaven generals decided to combine their forces for a third time as they prepared to launch their final assault. However, in order to do so, Andy and Pete were forced to delay their attack on Kevin's gates until the final campaign week of winter, as it was the only time when they would both be available to play together. As fate would have it, this also set up a suitably climactic make-or break battle for Barak Varr, and despite the fact that the outcome of this game would now have little overall effect on the campaign itself, the honour of the Dwarfs was on the line. But more importantly to the players, there were massive bragging rights up for grabs!

The results of the previous games in the War for Barak Varr would mean that the Skaven players would be able to field a combined total of 3000 points, whilst the stalwart Dwarfs would have a mere 2400 points with which to defend their Hold. The stage was set for a truly desperate battle…

The Final Battle

The furry tide of Skaven outnumbered the Dwarf host by almost two-to-one, but stoicism in the face of seemingly impossible odds has ever been Grimnir's legacy to the Dwarf race.

Wave after wave of Skaven attacks broke against the sturdy shields and Gromril armour of the Dwarfs, and though many valiant defenders fell in defence of their Hold, the rat-men were hurled back again and again. A giant creature, mutated in the deepest, darkest breeding pits, reared over the Dwarf battleline, tearing through their thick armour with unholy vigour, but not even this dread creature could break their spirit. As their numbers dwindled, the courage of the Skaven began to fail. At battle's end, the Dwarfs yet stood – bloodied, battered, but ultimately victorious.

Despite the overwhelming number of Skaven invaders, the Dwarf line holds firm.

WINTER CAMPAIGN TURN

Annotations

A Simon consolidates his empire but cannot quite drive the last of the Skaven from the shores of his empire.

B Matt's continued expansion succeeds in dividing the Tomb Kings' empire into two halves.

C Matt finally reclaims one of his mines from Andrew's Tomb Kings, although ironically it is exhausted no sooner than the last skeletal miner is slain.

D Andy's Skaven appear on the borders of Andrew's empire but they are resoundly defeated by the army of the Red Witch.

E Their uneasy truce long since put to one side, Simon and Kevin's armies clashed in a Storm of Magic game.

F The two Skaven players finally turn on one another, as Andy invades Pete's empire.

G The Grim Nebula attempts to storm Fozzrik's Gatehouse but is rebuffed.

H The High Elves attack the Empire forces at Hanging Rock, sweeping them from the top of the hill.

I Kevin's army returns to the surface, after seeing off the Skaven invaders from below.

J Fozzrik's Flying Fastness ends the campaign within the empire of the Chaos Warriors, gifting Tom 10 bonus relics.

Relic Counting

At the end of the campaign, each player must total up the number of relics they have, adding an extra one for every city, castle, mine or special feature they control. Players also get bonus relics for controlling Mount Bloodhorn, the Marshes of Madness, Morgheim and Fozzrik's Gatehouse, as well as the Flying Fastness. The player with the most relics starts the final game in the Flying Fastness, and then the players deploy on the two battlefields in descending order.

In our campaign this proved to be Tom, followed by Matt, Pete, Andy and Andrew. Simon, Chris and Kevin deployed on the second of the battlefields, meaning that the Flying Fastness was principally contested by the Forces of Destruction.

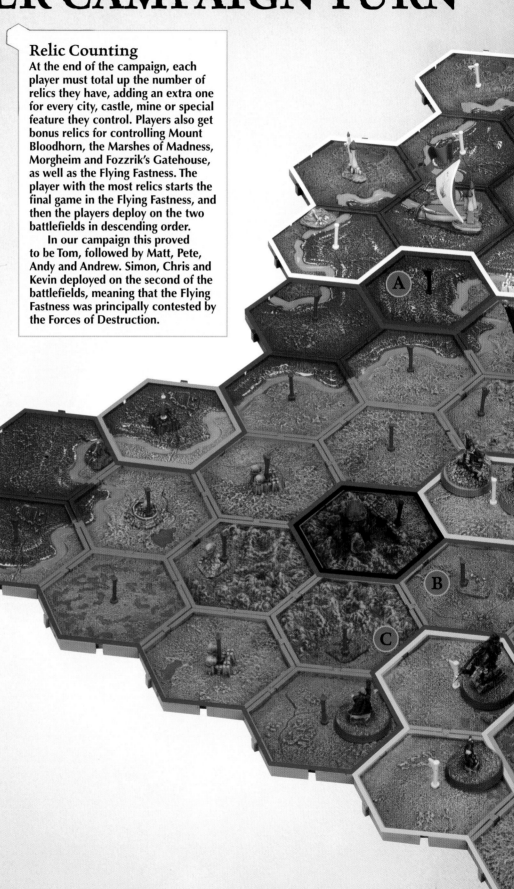

As icy temperatures and Ulric's wintery breath begin to make their freezing presence felt across the Badlands, only the foolish or the brave would dare to venture out into the cold to wage war.

Seasonal Rule
Winters in the Badlands are harsh affairs, as snow storms roll down from the Worlds Edge Mountains and strong winds powerful enough to hurl boulders blow unimpeded across the barren plains.

Roll a D6 at the start of each battle. On a 1-2 a blizzard sweeps over the battlefield and the maximum visibility is reduced to 24".

The bitter cold of winter's chill was as nothing compared to the bitter resentment held between the High Elves and the Dwarfs. So it was that the tenuous truce held between the lords of Barak Varr and Prince Aurelian Stormrider for the last nine months was broken at last in a showdown of epic proportions. Beneath the shadow of Fozzrik's Flying Fastness, Elf met Dwarf in the fury of a storm of magic. Hothar the Fey tapped into the power of the maelstrom, smiting Runesmiths with ruinous spells and transmuting Hammerers into the gold they so desired, but the tide turned against him when he lost control of the wild energy and was blasted unconscious. When he re-awoke, the Dwarfs stood bloodied but victorious and the exhausted Archmage was forced to retreat.

The season's fighting continued in earnest, with the Skaven of Clan Mange engaging in battle with the skeletal Khemrian army of the Red Witch. The battle raged to and fro, with both sides seeming to gain the upper hand before being force to relinquish their advantage to brutal counter-charges. Ultimately it was to be the unstoppable rampage of the Khemrian Warsphinx, *Usirian's Fury*, that broke the resolve of the Skaven hordes, striking down

their warlord and crushing his bodyguard beneath its enormous bulk.

The Skaven of Clan Mors were also seen abroad in the snow, fighting the undying legion of the dread Vampire Morivar Darkstalker for control of the Haunted Pass. The arcane warp technologies of the rat-men served them well in the opening stages of the battle, blasting apart a ferocious Varghulf and scything down the charging Blood Knights before they could put the cowardly vermin to flight. But the destructive intervention of Darkstalker and his terrifying steed caused such devastation amongst the Skaven ranks that their assault faltered in their moment of triumph. Both sides were forced to withdraw at battle's end, neither side left with strength enough to claim absolute victory.

Stiegfried Schweinsteiger led his men in a glorious defence of Fozzrik's Gatehouse against the unholy forces of the much-feared Lord Emberblade, who was accompanied by the Grim Nebula. The army of Chaos attacked the walls again and again, but each time the courage of the men of the Empire's held true and Emberblade's forces were repelled. Burning with fury that his plans were thwarted by such weaklings, the Tzeentch warlord was forced to call off the attack and regroup.

The Red Witch's Revenge

The Skaven and Tomb Kings clashed in a hard-fought contest set in the mountain passes near Naqqara. Andrew struck the first significant blow shortly after the game began. He slammed into Andy's Hell Pit Abomination with his Skeleton Chariots and, with the benefit of the Flaming Attacks granted by the Banner of Eternal Flame, rode into the terrible beast and ground its remains beneath their gilded wheels. Andy's army was far from squirting the musk of fear as his Warlord led a ferocious counter-attack that saw the chariots destroyed moments later. The large unit of Rat Ogres swung the battle back in Andy's favour, crushing a horde of Skeletons before crashing though to another unit behind. But the Rat Ogres were defeated in turn as Andrew augmented his warriors with powerful magic and routed the cowardly beasts. Andrew's Khemrian Warsphinx struck the telling blow, engaging Andy's Warlord and Clanrats in a fight they couldn't hope to win. After a series of Thundercrush attacks and a Killing Blow landed against Andy's Warlord, the mighty war statue emerged victorious, securing victory for the Red Witch.

Long has she harboured a thirst for revenge against the foul Skaven of Clan Mange, and now the Red Witch has seen an opportunity to lay her foe low.

With magic she has undone the spells of her foes, harvesting their souls for her casket. With arrow and skull she has reaped a tally upon the ratmen.

And with spear shaft and claw she has claimed the ultimate prize – the death of Warlord Hallscurry, spitted upon the blades of her defiant Tomb Guard.

Be gone back whence ye came foul Skaven!

- From the Red Witch to Warlord Hallscurry

"Your feeble attempts to bind the magical storm are as futile as your belief that beards complement your ugly faces!"

- A bitter Hothar the Fey

Stone vs. Sorcery

Simon's magical mastery served him well early in the game, and the Dwarfs' defences were often overwhelmed by the huge number of power dice available to the High Elves. Matters were made all the more desperate for Kevin when his Truthsayer first transformed into a frog and was then riddled with bowfire, and a rampaging Bonegrinder Giant brutally toe-punted his Runelord from atop his Arcane Fulcrum! Simon's dominance was to be short lived, however. His powerful unit of White Lions were overwhelmed and his elite Swordmasters routed moments later before a series of miscasts robbed him of an Archmage and Mage. Kev was able to pick off Simon's remaining spellcasters and emerge victorious.

THE STORMING OF THE FLYING FASTNESS

The campaign has reached its climax and Fozzrik's Flying Fastness is at last within reach of those that have fought so hard to claim it. The alliances of the past year no longer hold any meaning – now is the time to fight for ultimate glory.

Back to the Skies

After a year of roving across the skies of the Badlands, Fozzrik's Flying Fastness drifted down to land once more. The priceless treasures contained therein had drawn eight armies to war, each fighting for the mastery of Fozzrik's seminal creation.

But the first five armies to reach it were indeed lucky to have done so, for they had barely arrived before it took to the skies once more. Even as the other armies drew near, a vast expanse of the ground beneath them tore free and rose into the sky, following in the wake of the Flying Fastness as it climbed ever higher.

Blood has indeed been spilt over the Badlands. But the eight exhausted armies must gather their strength one last time for the final clash that will decide who lays claim to Fozzrik's Flying Fastness. The climactic battle is now at hand.

Scenario Special Rules

This scenario is designed for five or more players. The first five players will be fighting on the Fozzrik's Flying Fastness battlefield. Any additional players will begin on the Floating Rocks battlefield, though they can still earn the right to challenge for Fozzrik's Flying Fastness, as explained later.

Each player chooses his force using the army list from a Warhammer army book, to an equal points value agreed before the game. If playing as part of the campaign, each player may also include his leader and both of his lieutenants for free. You may also select any number of Heroes of Legend and Regiments of Renown from your army rosters – this is the final battle and the time for the best of the best to step forward – though you must pay the points for them.

Deployment

Before forces are deployed, each player must select their starting locations. If playing as part of a campaign, the player with the most relics (see page 74) deploys first, setting up inside Fozzrik's Flying Fastness. The remaining players then take turns to choose their starting locations and set up, based on their number of relics in descending order. If two players have the same number of relics, then the player with the most campaign tiles will deploy before the other. If this is also a draw, then roll off. If you wish to play this as a standalone game, then roll off between all the players to decide the order of deployment. If the game includes more than five players, follow the steps above and continue deploying on the Floating Rocks battlefield.

The games on both battlefields should be played simultaneously, but players need not wait for the same turn on each table to be completed before continuing. This is intentionally lenient in order for each game to flow nicely, but it helps to try and play at a steady pace.

Adrift on the Tides of Magic

The maelstrom of magical energy that is lifting the battlefield even as the battle takes place has also torn the Arcane Fulcrums from the ground. These floating rocks move around the battlefield as the fight rages below them, neither blocking line of sight nor impeding movement.

At the start of each compulsory movement phase, each floating rock will move D6" in a random direction determined by a scatter dice. If this takes the rock into contact with a table edge, then the raging gale of magic that is elevating the battlefield will cast it back into play – simply 'bounce' the floating rock back onto the battlefield as if the table edge were a wall.

Should any floating rocks collide, then any Wizard currently occupying the Arcane Fulcrums atop each rock must pass an Initiative test or fall to the battlefield below and suffer a Strength 10 hit.

FOZZRIK'S FLYING FASTNESS

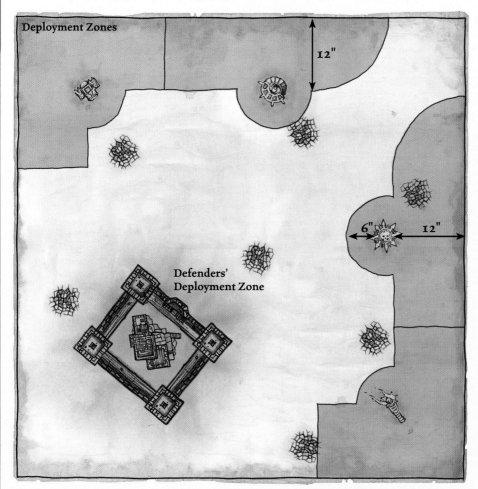

Deployment Zones

12"

6"   12"

Defenders'
Deployment Zone

The Battlefield

This scenario is played on a 6' x 6' table. Place a complete Warhammer Fortress or similar terrain piece on the battlefield to represent the walls of Fozzrik's Flying Fastness. Place an Arcane Fulcrum, Witchfate Tor, or other suitably impressive terrain piece in the centre of the fortress courtyard to represent the primary fulcrum. Finally, place four Arcane Fulcrums 12" in from a table edge or corner.

Objectives

The four towers and primary fulcrum are all objectives.

Deployment

The player who set up first (see opposite), may deploy anywhere within the fortress, occupying any of wall, tower or gate sections as normal. This player must also place a Wizard atop the primary Arcane Fulcrum.

The other players then take it in turns to deploy their armies. Units may be placed anywhere within 12" of their chosen table edge, or within 6" of their Arcane Fulcrum. They must also place a Wizard atop their Arcane Fulcrum.

THE FLOATING ROCKS

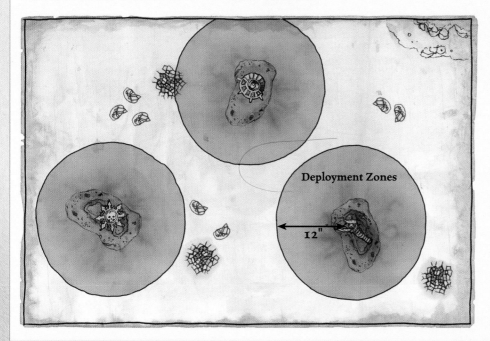

Deployment Zones

12"

The Battlefield

This scenario is played on a standard 6' x 4' table. Set up any terrain as normal.

Deployment

Before anyone deploys, each player takes it in turn to place a floating rock. Starting with the player who sets up first, place a floating rock at least 6" away from any table edge. This rock now moves D6" in a random direction determined by a scatter dice. Each player now places their floating rocks as above, but no closer than 24" to another rock before rolling to scatter.

Each player now deploys his army. Units may be placed anywhere within 12" of their floating rock. They must also place a Wizard atop their Arcane Fulcrum.

Multi-player Madness!

For both games to run smoothly, these scenarios use the Battle Royale turn sequence special rules from page 406 of Warhammer. As per these rules, each player will take their turn in accordance with the order in which they deployed. i.e. The player with the most relics, who deployed first, inside Fozzrik's Flying Fastness, will move first each turn.

Should another player arrive on the battlefield later in the game (see below), they will join the end of the turn queue and move last. If two or more players arrive in the same turn, use the order in which they successfully cast the spell to dictate the order of their arrival and subsequent turn sequence as normal.

CANTRIP

Fozzrik's Freight-fleecing Flimflam

Cast on 25+

Dominance. *It was with this spell that Fozzrik was able to amass such a vast collection of arcane treasures, summoning the contents of hidden vaults or entire baggage trains to his Flying Fastness.*

Fozzrik's Freight-fleecing Flimflam is an **augment** spell that targets all friendly units on the Floating Rocks battlefield. The target units are immediately removed from the table and will arrive on the Fozzrik's Flying Fastness battlefield at the start of the next game turn. Firstly, deploy the Wizard that cast the spell, then place all other units anywhere within 12" of this model, provided that no models are within 1" of another model or impassable terrain, and are deployed outside of the fortress walls.

This epic confrontation sees the culmination of a year of war, and the declaration of an ultimate campaign champion. It is fitting that this climactic battle is therefore nothing short of a maelstrom of gaming madness, combining elements of Storm of Magic, Siege special rules, and even the ability for an army to transfer from one table to another!

In order for these battles to operate in this manner and for a winner to be crowned, it is necessary to incorporate a number of scenario special rules:

Divided Loyalties

With Fozzrik's Flying Fastness within their grasp, every general is out for himself. As a result, any previous alliances broken. Players are free to make alliances with (and are encouraged to backstab) each other, but are always treated as being enemies for the purposes of spells, shooting and combat. Players are free to target enemies that are fighting in combat with each other – unless these attacks use a template, simply randomise hits between the combatants.

We Stand Alone

No general can expect reinforcements. The player who is defending Fozzrik's Flying Fastness must deploy his entire army within the fortress walls or occupying them. He may not choose to organise a Relief Force.

Hungry only for Battle

The armies that made it to Fozzrik's Flying Fastness had barely arrived before it took off once more, so starvation rolls are ignored for this scenario – the player that is defending the fortress will already have his hands full fighting off the four enemy armies that are attacking the walls!

No Time to Think – Only to Act!

As mentioned above, the five armies fighting on this battlefield have had little time to deploy for battle, let alone arrange any preliminary bombardments or plan any sneaky tricks. As a result, the Pre-battle phase is also ignored for this scenario.

We Came Prepared

In preparation for claiming Fozzrik's Flying Fastness, each army came prepared to storm the walls if necessary. But no amount of careful planning could have prepared even the most canny general for the limited time they would have before they would be thrust into the thick of an epic battle. No players may spend any points on Siege Equipment, but every army is assumed to have armed their war machines with Siege Ammunition. In addition, every unit is assumed to have ladders or grappling hooks with which to attack the fortress walls. These rules apply even if they began the game on the Floating Rocks battlefield.

Each side also has access to the Cataclysm Siege spells (see right), which are treated as any other Cataclysm spells.

Game Length

The player who controls the primary Arcane Fulcrum on the Fozzrik's Flying Fastness battlefield rolls a dice at the end of each game turn, starting with the end of game turn 6. Add the turn number to the dice roll. If the score is 12 or more, then the battle ends immediately. If the total is less than 12 then the battle continues for at least one more game turn. This applies to the games on both battlefields.

It is likely that the game on the Floating Rocks battlefield will be further ahead on their turn count, but for the purposes of the game ending it simply gives those players an extra turn or two to try and join the main game on the Fozzrik's Flying Fastness battlefield.

Victory Conditions

The Storming of the Flying Fastness scenario has special victory conditions, as follows. Players can only win the game by controlling the objectives located on the Fozzrik's Flying Fastness battlefield. Whichever player has the most objectives under their control by the time the game ends will win the campaign!

In the case of two or more players controlling the same number of objectives, the player who also controls the most Arcane Fulcrums will win. If this is also a draw, then control of the primary Arcane Fulcrum will be the deciding factor.

Designer's Notes

The special victory conditions of this scenario mean that if you begin the game on the Floating Rocks battlefield, your overriding priority should be to reach the Fozzrik's Flying Fastness battlefield at all costs – only by doing this can you bring yourself back into contention and start contesting the objectives. In order to do so, you must achieve Dominance and cast the special Cantrip, *Fozzrik's Freight-fleecing Flimflam* (see left). Remember though that if one of your opponents manages to do so, their army is immediately removed from play, leaving a cunning commander free to take advantage of the situation during that Magic phase. With careful use of Cantrips, it's even possible to gain Dominance and follow suit later in the same Magic phase! But be careful – if you lose all of your spellcasters, you can end up stranded on the Floating Rocks table…

CATACLYSM SIEGE SPELLS

LORE OF FIRE

Towering Inferno
Cast on 25+

Presence. *Binding the Wind of Aqshy into the very stone of the walls before him, the Wizard gestures and the magical energy is unleashed as a torrent of raging flame.*

Towering Inferno is a **direct damage** spell that can be cast on any tower, gate or wall section within 24". Every model occupying that building section suffers a Strength 4 hit with the Flaming Attacks special rule. Remember that you may also re-roll failed To Wound rolls with Flaming Attacks against models that are occupying a building.

LORE OF BEASTS

Kadon's Bestial Surge
Cast on 25+

Presence. *Uttering a spell that Kadon himself first devised, the Wizard infuses a Scroll of Binding with all the savage energy of Ghur, magnifying the target creature's animal fury.*

Remains in play. *Kadon's Bestial Surge* is an **augment** spell that can be cast on any bound monster, or unit of bound monsters within 24"; it may even be cast on the Wizard himself if he is also a bound monster. For the duration of the spell, the targets double their Strength characteristic. In addition, the player may direct the monster's attacks against a fortress section, causing a breach on any rolls of a 6 to hit.

LORE OF LIGHT

Dissolution of Stone
Cast on 25+

Presence. *Piercing the walls of the fortress with his mystic gaze, the wizard's will unbinds the mortar that holds them intact. What happens next is inevitable.*

Dissolution of Stone is a **direct damage** spell that can be cast on any tower, gate or wall section within 24". That fortress section is now breached for the rest of the game.

LORE OF METAL

Gehenna's Golden Gun
Cast on 25+

Presence. *The Wizard drops a golden nugget to the floor, summoning the artifice of his race to transmute the enchanted ingot into a mighty weapon of war.*

Remains in play. *Gehenna's Golden Gun* is a **summoning** spell with a range of 12". The summoned unit must be a war machine, such as a Cannon or Bolt Thrower, chosen from the same Warhammer army book you used to write your army list. The model's points value is ignored – you may summon any war machine normally available to your army.

No upgrades may be taken for a war machine summoned this way, but it is assumed to be equipped with Siege Ammunition (as appropriate), and always hits with both Flaming and magical attacks.

Note that *Gehenna's Golden Gun* is a remains in play spell, and may therefore be dispelled at a later stage. Should this happen, the war machine is removed from play.

LORE OF HEAVENS

Thorsen's Howling Gale
Cast on 25+

Presence. *Gesturing towards his enemies as they cower behind their walls, the wizard summons a blistering gale, hurling any not strong enough to hold on from the ramparts.*

Thorsen's Howling Gale is a **magic missile** that can be cast on any tower, gate or wall section within 24". Every model occupying that building section must pass a Strength test or fall to their deaths as they are hurled from the castle walls. No saves of any kind are allowed.

LORE OF LIFE

Wall of Vines
Cast on 25+

Presence. *Summoning forth the Wind of Ghyran to undo the damage done to the fortress' broken walls, the Wizard seals the breach with a thick mesh of tangled vines.*

Wall of Vines is an **augment** spell that can be cast on any breached tower, gate or wall section within 24". The damage to that fortress section is repaired and it is no longer treated as being breached.

LORE OF SHADOW

Mist of Shadows
Cast on 25+

Presence. *The Wizard envelopes the battlements with choking cloud of magical darkness. When the mysterious fog dissipates, there is no one to be seen.*

Mist of Shadows is a **hex** spell that can be cast on any tower, gate or wall section within 24". Every model occupying that building section is immediately removed from the table and replaced anywhere on the battlefield within 24" of the Wizard, provided that no model from the unit is within 1" of another unit or impassable terrain. The affected unit may be returned to play facing any direction, but in a formation of the owning player's choosing. This spell can be used to remove enemy units from combat – any units left without an opponent can immediately reform.

LORE OF DEATH

Soul Harvest
Cast on 25+

Presence. *Uttering fell words of power, the Wizard suffuses the stone of the fortress with a sickly aura. Those that fall beneath this dread emanation lose more than just their lives.*

Remains in play. *Soul Harvest* is an **augment** spell that can be cast on any tower, gate or wall section within 24" that is occupied by friendly models. For each unsaved wound the unit occupying the nominated fortress section inflicts in close combat, they will immediately regain a single Wound suffered earlier in the battle. The owning player is free to distribute these regained wounds between the unit and any characters that may have joined them.

Note that should the occupying unit leave the nominated fortress section, the spell will automatically end.

AMIDST THE FLOATING ROCKS

The Forces of Order must fight it out between themselves, the winner joining the armies of Destruction in the cataclysmic battle for Fozzrik's Flying Fastness. However, the victor must act quickly, or else the prize will be lost before he arrives.

Kevin's Dwarfs, Simon's High Elves and Chris' Empire had the least amount of relics and so were relegated to the Floating Rocks table. We gave the players an hour's grace before the main game started and they played at a frantic rate, hoping that they could gain Dominance and cast the cantrip before the other battle was done. For the Dwarfs, we said that the spell was placed into a rune (which worked exactly like casting a cantrip) to at least give them a shot at winning! Simon started the battle in an aggressive manner, his Manticore flying ahead, desperate to get into combat with the enemy wizards. He also targeted his bolt throwers at the Arcane Fulcrums, hoping that one of the enemy Wizards would fail their 3+ ward saves and allow him to quickly steal an objective and cast the Cantrip, whilst the others were still formulating their own plans.

As it was, the Empire gained the upper hand. In a crafty move by the warrior-poet, Chris slew the High Elf Mage with a cannon shot and then summoned a Wizard, who teleported onto the Arcane Fulcrum before Simon could react. With Dominance achieved, even Kevin's Runesmith couldn't prevent the Battle Wizard casting the cantrip and teleporting off the table with the Empire army in tow.

Dominance

A cannon ball and skilled use of the Magic phase were all that was needed for Chris to gain the upper hand. Whilst the other two players went for a more traditional means of knocking Wizards off fulcrums, Chris Peach was uncharacteristically sneaky, and lulled Simon into a false sense of security. After all, he only seemed to have one wizard on the battlefield.

Never underestimate the summoning spell in a Storm of Magic game!

Annotations

A Beast fight! Kevin and Simon's monsters started scrapping early in the battle. Simon would have preferred to feed Aurelian's Griffon on Wizard or Runesmith, but Kevin was wise to the ploy and sent out his Chimera to stop him.

B The High Elves' acid-spitting Hydra was a constant annoyance for the Dwarfs, whose heavy armour struggled against the acrid liquid.

C Riled by the magical tempest, Kev's Runesmith was hammering his Ancestor Rune with a wild fervour. The Ancestor Rune of Grimnir was struck time and time again, causing the deaths of many High Elves, a few men of the Empire, causing two miscasts as well.

D Chris used his ranged weapons over his combat troops, as he wanted to keep them fresh, so he'd still have big units should he reach the Fastness.

THE LAST BATTLE

It all comes down to this final clash of armies. After a year of war, of empires conquered, and realms sundered, ultimate victory is in sight at last. But who will take Fozzrik's Flying Fastness and lay claim to the secrets inside?

From the west, the Skaven came. Clan Mange, now no longer in thrall to the Screaming One since his destruction at Fozzrik's Gatehouse, shrugged off any pretence of an alliance with Clan Fawsquikk. Not surprisingly, Pete was of the same mind, and with the two Skaven armies deploying next to each other, acts of aggression were inevitable from the start.

Meanwhile, Tom's Chaos Army, who had the most relics, started the game in the Flying Fastness itself. In theory, Tom had the advantage by starting on the objectives. However, he wasn't so sure, knowing that his smallish force had a lot of walls and towers to man, and that everybody (feuding Skaven aside) would be out for his blood. To the south, marched the Tomb Kings under the dominion of their new liege, and to the west, more Undead in the form of Matt's Vampire Counts were ready to assault the fortress.

The battle started with the armies advancing on the ensorcelled castle. Tom's army looked on from the battlements as hordes of Skaven, legions of Skeletons and a Zombie Dragon closed in on the fortress.

Tom started the Magic phase by trying to cast *Purple Sun of Xereus*, but this was wisely dispelled by his opponents. Andy placed a *Pit of the Underworld* under the Fortress, but would have to wait to see if the strategy bore fruit in a later phase. Pete kicked off by trying to turn Andy's Clanrats into, er… Clanrats! Alas, the unit proved too big but they still died in droves. Skaven fighting against Skaven? This didn't seem right! Or maybe it did… Andy tried to quickly forge another alliance, 'at least until Tom is out of the castle' but his pleas fell upon 'death' ears. Meanwhile, Andrew had gained dominance and had cast *Return of the Golden Age* – the White Dwarf editor had his game face on!

Annotations

A Matt's Undead led the charge on the fortress, his Vargulf and Blood Knights striking early but they were repelled.

B Tom's Chaos Knights engaged the Skeleton spearmen, confident of victory. That was until Andrew cast *Return of the Golden Age*. This changed the odds somewhat, but could Tom's Chaos Knights still hold off the skeletal legion?

C Morivar Darkstalker, Matt's Vampire Lord, entered the Flying Fortress after emptying it of the previous occupants by using the *Mist of Shadows* spell.

D Andy's Ghorgon charged the enemy Grey Seer, in response to Pete's earlier magical attack with the *Dreaded Thirteenth Spell*. The Grey Seer would have been slain many times over, but for the 3+ ward save of the Arcane Fulcrum.

"IT SHALL BE MINE"

Even as the armies warred outside, two Lords prepared to battle.

Skel did not fear the corpse-creature before him, neither was the Vampire Lord intimidated by the Chaos pawn who stood defiant.

Flaming sword struck cursed blade, as two of the most powerful beings in the world fought along the battlements of the fastness, all the while a raging magical tempest blew overhead.

The two Lords duelled, but at the last, Tzeentch abandoned his champion, and the Vampire struck him down with a fatal blow, lopping off the Chaos Lord's head. Darkstalker was victorious but had he done enough to lay claim to the entire fortress?

While the Skaven ineffectually fought amongst themselves and the Tomb Kings dawdled, the Vampire Counts kept their eye on the prize. Clever use of his spells, specifically the *Mist of Shadows*, had gained the Vampire Lord easy ingress into the Flying Fastness.

The spell had displaced Tom's Hellcannon, Chaos Ogres and Chaos Sorcerer out of the tower. Matt caused even more havoc by placing the Ogres in front of Andrew's marble Necrosphinx, the Chaos Sorcerer facing Matt's own Black Dragon and the Hellcannon in front of the Red Witch. The Vampires were playing dirty!

Meanwhile, the Skaven were attacking the north wall. Andy had decided to ignore Pete's aggression as much as possible and concentrate on breaching the castle. His Rat Ogres and Chimera attacked Tom's Chaos Warriors and the Great Chaos Spawn. The Chaos Warriors had the benefit of the fortress walls, but failed their Fear test and so were reduced to WS 1. The Rat Ogres also failed their own Fear test so both sides were rolling 4s to hit. As it was, Tom won the combat by slaying four Rat Ogres, thereby blunting the Skaven attack.

However, things were going to be far from predictable with not one, but two, Screaming Bells on the battlefield! In the following turn Andy struck his despoiled bell, the deafening peals rang out across the battle causing a 'Wall of Unholy Sound'. This gave the majority of Andy's Skaven an extra attack, but more importantly every building within 24" would collapse on a roll of 4+. And, yes, that included at least half of the Flying Fastness. But, despite all the rolling, the only structure to collapse was the northern tower – the Chaos Warriors occupying it suddenly found themselves on the ground amidst a load of rubble! In the previous phase, Tom's Daemon Prince had moved from the castle to attack the Skaven lines, but failed to make the charge. With the Grim Nebula stranded, this meant that the Hell Pit Abomination nearby could have a fight after all!

Across the board the Necrosphinx was busy slaughtering Tom's Chaos Ogres. But the largest monster fight had to be between Matt's Vampire Lord and Tom's Chaos Lord – the victor could well take the castle and the entire campaign.

Warriors of the Golden Age

Before the gates of the Flying Fastness a titanic combat was taking place. The Chaos Knights charged into the Skeleton Warriors, but they were soon bolstered by a Giant, who, in turn had a Doomwheel ram into its back. The Giant was the first to fall, its rear scorched by bolts of warp lightning. Quite dead, it then fell onto the Skeletons and Chaos Knights causing multiple deaths in both units. The Chaos Knights were the ultimate losers though, forced to flee from the Skeletons, who were enhanced by the *Return of the Golden Age* spell.

Better Late than Never

Schweinsteiger's army appeared at the start of the third turn. At this point the other five armies were spread out across a good deal of the battlefield, forcing Chris to deploy in the far west, as this was the only area large enough to cope with his materialising army that didn't break any of the rules conditions. This put the Empire army directly behind Pete's Skaven. If Chris wanted to win the campaign he would have to fight through Pete's army and then get into the castle. A tall order, but the warrior-poet was always up for a challenge (and new material for his ditties). The appearance of a large Empire army in his rear forced Pete to stop fighting Andy and concentrate on the men – there would be more blood spilled this day!

And the Winner is…

Despite losing their Chaos Lord in a dramatic fight with the Vampire, the forces of Tzeentch won the day. At battle's end Tom's Chaos Warriors still held three objectives to Matt's two. Fozzrik's Flying Fastness and all the secrets it contained were now in the hands of Tzeentch and if that isn't a frightening prospect, I don't know what is!

Even then, things didn't end simply. With Mawhrin Skel dead – his body still laying upon the ramparts – it was his Sorcerer, Ifrit Skybound, who took control and won the campaign. Maybe that was the plan all along…

So Tom is crowned Campaign Champion and gets to rule the Badlands, for now anyway. In retrospect, Tom was deserving of the overall victory, as his empire was the largest at the time of the final battle, and he won most of the games he played.

'It's been hard fought,' admits Tom, 'but brilliant fun. There's nothing like playing in such an involved campaign. What helped me was keeping my empire in a solid block and not over-stretching myself. And when I did strike, I went for important tiles, like Stormhenge. Right, when do we start our next campaign? My Tyranids need to see some action!'

SIEGE BATTLES

With cities, castles and the odd flying fortress abound, sieging was always going to play a strong part of the campaign. So we asked Jervis Johnson if he could come up with some Siege rules and it just so happened he some to hand.

Jervis: I've always had a soft spot for siege games, and over the years I've attacked and defended more than a few mighty fortresses. What this has taught me is that its important to keep the rules used for siege games as short as possible; nobody wants to have to learn another thirty pages of rules before they get to launch their assault! So, when the new version of Warhammer was released, I was intrigued by the idea of coming up with a set of siege rules that would fit onto only a few pages, so that players could get fighting as quickly as possible. The rules on the following pages are the result of those deliberations.

Although, they are presented here for this campaign, feel free to try them out whenever you want assault a castle!

THE FORTRESS

In order to fight a siege game you will need a fortress to fight over. For the purposes of the rules that follow I've assumed that you have a Warhammer Fortress from the Warhammer Scenery range. If you're using anything other than a Warhammer Fortress you may need to make some slight adjustments to the rules below, but I'm sure you'll easily be able to muddle on by.

THE ARMIES

Each player chooses an army from a Warhammer Armies army list, to an equal points value agreed before the game. Roll randomly to decide who will be defending the Warhammer Fortress after you've picked armies. The attacker has their full army. The defender must split his units into a defence force and a relief force. Both forces must have at least one non-character unit. Note that this means its possible to fight a siege simply using two armies picked for a normal game – no advance preparation is necessary!

Siege Points

Each player gets a number of siege points equal to the points value of their army. Siege points may be spent to include siege equipment in an army, chosen from the

attacker's & defender's siege equipment lists later on. So if you were fighting a siege with two 2000 point armies, each player would get an extra 2000 points to spend on siege equipment. A selection of Siege equipment is shown is a few pages time.

THE BATTLEFIELD

The defender sets up the Warhammer Fortress, an example set up is shown on the map below. The attacker sets up the terrain outside the fortress using any of the methods described in the Warhammer.

DEPLOYMENT

At the start of the battle place three objective markers on the fortress. Anything can be used as a marker – a small coin is ideal. The attacker places the 1st marker, then the defender places the 2nd marker, and the attacker places the 3rd marker. Markers must be placed on a fortress wall, gate or tower sections. You may not place two markers in the same section. The position of the marker within the section is not important.

After objectives have been placed the defending force deploys inside the fortress and on its walls. Then the attacker deploys outside the fortress more than 8" away from the walls.

SIEGE DEPLOYMENT

The Battlefield

The defender can normally set up the fortress in any formation he wants, providing he has enough castle sections. One side of the table is always the defenders, so you don't have to form a compete perimeter. A Warhammer Fortress can be placed in the set-up shown on the right, to give a good defensive layout and ensure an exciting game.

The Relief Force

The Relief Force will arrive later in the battle. The table side it will arrive on will depend on a D6 roll: 1-2 on the left of the fortress; 3-4 opposite the fortress; 5-6 right of the fortress.

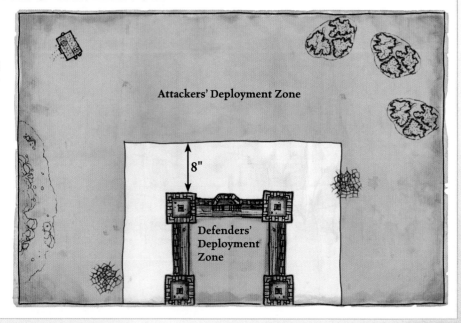

Attackers' Deployment Zone

8"

Defenders' Deployment Zone

Complicated Combats

The Chaos Warriors (A) are assaulting the wall section held by the Greatswords (B). Before the attack begins in earnest the Greatswords got to stand and shoot by throwing rocks.

In the assault, the Chaos player makes his 'assault party' from both units (A & C) by taking both champions and the remaining eight from unit C (as these will not suffer from WS and I penalties). The Empire player could do the same with the Swordsmen (D) but stays with ten Greatswords, rather than mixing it up. In the fight the Chaos Warriors slay seven. The Greatswords strike back, killing an impressive eight with their double-handed swords. The Chaos player's total remains at seven, but the Empire player gets a +1 for being a defender with an occupied connected tower (D) so his total is nine. Both Chaos Warrior units must take a Break test at -2.

The Starvation Roll

The defender has been besieged for some time, so will have suffered casualties. Before deployment, the attacker rolls 1D6 for each model in the fortress; they suffer 1 wound on a roll of 5+, with no armour saves allowed. The defender should update their roster to reflect the losses suffered, and then deploy their army.

Splitting Up

Defending units may be split up to occupy more than one section of the fortress when they deploy. Each part of the unit operates on its own (i.e. as a separate unit) for the duration of the battle; they may not join back up again after they have been split up. Command groups may be put in any unit, and may be split up if desired.

The Relief Force

At the start of the battle the defender must hold back a proportion of his army, who will turn up during the battle as reinforcements. No starvation roll is made for models in the relief force.

Roll 2D6 at the start of each of the defender's turns, starting with Turn 2. Add the turn number to the score. On a roll of 10 or more the entire relief force arrives.

The relief force enters play in the same manner as reinforcements as described on page 27 of Warhammer. Roll a dice; on a roll of 1-2 it arrives on the table edge to the left of the fortress; on a roll of 3-4 it arrives on the table edge opposite the fortress; and on a roll of 5-6 it arrives on the table edge to the right of the fortress.

Important: Units from the relief force cannot enter or attack fortress sections from the outside (they don't have ladders or such like). They can move or attack sections from inside the fortress.

PRE-BATTLE PHASE

The following 'pre-battle phase' takes place after both sides have deployed, but before the first turn of the battle begins.

1 **Defensive Artillery Fire:** Roll two dice for each defending stone thrower or cannon in the fortress. Each roll of 6 destroys one attacking war machine that is in range and sight of the defending war machine.

2 **Attacking Artillery Fire:** Roll two dice for each attacking stone thrower, cannon or bolt thrower. Re-roll all rolls of 6. If the re-roll is 1-3 the attack destroys one defending war machine that is in range and sight of the attacking war machine, and if it is 4-6 it causes a breach in a wall section that is in range and sight. Breached wall sections are much easier to assault (see below). Bolt throwers cannot breach wall sections and will count re-rolls of 4+ as a miss.

3 **Defensive Missile Fire:** Defending troops that didn't shoot in phase 1 may now shoot twice, yes really! Artillery that shoots in this phase and suffers a misfire may not be used in the first turn of the battle (do not roll on the misfire table).

4 **Assault Commences:** Battle starts with the Attackers first turn – bless your weapons or call to your dark gods for the siege will be bloody!

MOVING AROUND THE FORTRESS

Use the standard building rules, counting each wall section, gate or tower as a separate building. Units in one section can move to a connected section that is unoccupied, or can assault connected sections in the Combat phase (if they win they capture the section they attacked, if they lose they stay where they are). Friendly units in adjacent sections may swap places. Any unit can garrison a fortress section; it is not limited to infantry and monstrous infantry.

Towers

Tower and gate sections may be occupied by a war machine as well as a defending unit. Place the war machine on the tower or gateway, and measure its attacks from this location. If the enemy attack the section with missile fire, then they can either shoot at the war machine, or the other unit in the section. Crew models may be selected to defend the section if it is attacked. The war machine is destroyed if the attackers ever capture the section.

Gateways

Units can move through gate sections held by their own side as if they were clear ground, and may declare charges at enemy units on the other side of a gate as if they could see them. This allows the defender's to 'sally forth' through gate sections.

SHOOTING FROM THE FORTRESS

Up to ten models plus a war machine are allowed to shoot from each fortress section.

ATTACKING THE FORTRESS

Units attacking from the outside of the fortress are assumed to have ladders or grappling hooks that allow them to assault fortress sections. Unless they are flyers, models attacking this way must halve their Weapon Skill and Initiative, rounding down. Note that units attacking from siege towers or into a breached sections do so normally.

Fortress Defence Bonus

A defending unit in a fortress section adds +1 to its combat resolution score for each connected section occupied by a friendly unit. This is an exception to the rule that says that combat resolution modifiers are not used when assaulting buildings (and note that any other modifiers are not used).

Connected Sections

In the Close Combat phase a unit in a fortress section can be assaulted by one unit that is outside the fortress, plus one extra enemy unit from each connected fortress section. In theory this means that a unit could be assaulted by up to three separate enemy units (one outside and one from the connected sections on either side). However, the maximum number of models that may fight in the assault remains at 10 models per side; if the attacker assaults from several sections he may choose the ten models from any of the units that are assaulting.

Into the Breach

Sometimes fortress sections will be 'breached' (see the pre battle phase above). Keep a note of which sections have been breached, or do as we do and mark them with a pile of rocks (well, pebbles really!).

Breached sections are much harder to defend. To represent this, if the attacker wins a combat against a breached fortress section, then the defender is forced out even if they don't break. Place the defending unit outside the fortress section using the rules for abandoning a

building. Note that a defender may retreat into an adjacent unoccupied fortress section if desired. If it is impossible for the unit to abandon the section, then it is destroyed. The fortress section is then occupied by the attacking unit.

Note that a fortress section may never be destroyed or removed, only breached. If a spell, magic item or other special rule that requires you to remove a building is cast on a castle section, it is instead breached.

Rocks

Units occupying a fortress section count as being armed with heavy rocks with the profile below, in addition to the weapons they usually carry. Rocks may be used to 'stand and fire' against attackers, unless the attacker is a flyer or is making his assault from a connected fortress section or siege tower. Rocks always hit on a 5+, no matter what the ballistic skill of the model dropping it, and no matter what modifiers would normally apply. Even units that are not normally allowed to stand and fire (such as Undead, for example, or war machine crew) may do so with rocks.

Type	Range	Strength	Special
Rocks	1"	3	Quick To Fire

WINNING THE SIEGE

The game ends at the end of turn five. The attacker wins if they have captured all three objectives, and the defender wins if the attacker only has control of one objective (or none at all!). If the attacker controls two objectives, then victory points are used to determine the winner.

Relieved!

The defender wins immediately if a unit of 5 or more models from the relief force enters the fortress through a gateway before the end of turn five. Note that the relief force unit needs to enter through the gateway – flying or tunnelling into the courtyard, or using any other method of movement, doesn't count! Also note that to move through the gateway, the gate section needs to be occupied by a defending unit, to open the gate.

SIEGE EQUIPMENT

Each side gets a number of siege points equal to the points value of their army with which to purchase siege equipment. There are two lists of siege equipment, one for the attacker and one for the defender. Each player can choose any items from their list, up to the points value they are allowed to take. Items can be taken multiple times if you wish and have the siege points to pay for them.

Inventing your own Siege Equipment

The list of siege equipment we included with this article is fairly limited, covering those items of Siege Equipment available in the Warhammer range, plus a small selection of other items that do not need to be represented by models. However, it is very easy to come up with additional pieces of equipment for the list, and creative groups of players can have a lot of fun expanding on what we've included here. This is exactly what the players did in their campaign; I let the players know that if they came up with an interesting idea for a piece of siege equipment – especially ones that reflected the nature and character of the army that used them – then I'd be happy to give them a points value and would allow the player to use them in his games. Andy Hall proved especially cunning at devising fiendish Skaven siege engines and devilish ploys (undermining foundations and gaseous caverns were also mentioned), much to the consternation of his bewildered foes!

ATTACKER'S SIEGE EQUIPMENT

Siege Tower   1000 points

Siege Towers count as a 'building' that can move. Siege towers can be occupied by units in the same manner as a normal building.

Siege Tower Movement: Siege towers are jury-built and rickety. Roll a D6 before moving them:

1   *Wheel Falls Off!* May not move this turn while the wheel is stuck back on again.

2-6 *'Ere we Go!* Move 8"

Siege towers may not charge, wheel or reform (i.e., they always move straight forward), but are allowed to move into contact with fortress sections. If they do so then any unit that is in the tower is allowed to make an assault just as if it had charged the fortress.

Once in contact with the fortress it counts as a 'connected fortress section' for the remainder of the game. Note that once in contact with the fortress a siege tower cannot move again (or be driven back if models occupying it lose a combat), and are treated in all ways as part of the fortress. Also note that the defenders can attack the siege tower and may be able to capture it.

Battering Ram   500 points

Battering Rams count as a chariot that use the following profile.

	M	WS	BS	S	T	W	I	A	LD
Battering Ram	1D6+2	-	-	6	5	-	-	-	-
5 Crew	-	3	3	3	-	-	3	1	7

Special Rules: Unbreakable.

Fixed Axle: Battering rams may not charge, wheel or reform (i.e., they always move straight forward), but are allowed to move into contact with fortress sections.

Batter: Once in contact with the fortress it can start to batter the walls. Roll at the start of each combat phase in which the battering ram is in contact with a fortress section to see if a breach is made. The battering ram will make a breach on a roll of 5+. Add +1 to the dice roll if trying to 'breach' a gate section. A section can be battered by a battering ram while another unit launches an assault on it.

Steam Tank Battering Ram   250 points
Empire only.

An Empire Steam Tank may be given a battering ram for 250 points. If a Steam Tank fitted with a ram is within 1" of the fortress it can start to batter the walls. Roll at the start of each Close Combat phase to see if a breach is made. The attack does not cost any steam points. The ram will breach on a roll of 5+. Add +1 to the dice roll if trying to 'breach' a gate section.

Monstrous Battering Clubs   250 points per unit

Any monster or unit of monstrous infantry can be given clubs or similar equipment with which to batter the walls of the fortress. If a unit equipped with a monstrous club is within 1" of the fortress it can start to batter the walls. Roll at the start of each Close Combat phase to see if a breach is made in the section. The attack is made instead of it's normal attacks. The monster or monstrous infantry will make a breach on a roll of 5+. Add +1 to the dice roll if trying to 'breach' a gate section.

Siege Ammunition   100 points per unit

Stone throwers and cannons that have siege ammunition that hit a fortress section in a Shooting phase will breach it on a roll of 6+. Note that this happens during normal play, not in the pre-battle phase.

Hasty Assault   Half total siege points

If the attacker makes a hasty assault then all starvation rolls suffer a -1 modifier. However, the defender may not start rolling for his relief force to arrive until turn 4, and the force suffers a -1 penalty to its arrival roll. A hasty assault cost the attacker half of his starting number of siege points.

Undermines   250 points

The attacker can attempt to undermine the fortress walls. For each undermine that is taken the attacker can roll an additional two dice in the Attacking Artillery Fire pre-battle phase. However, undermines cannot destroy defending war machines (ignore rolls of 1-3).

Restless Dead   1000 points

Vampire Counts only.

The attacker binds the departed souls of those that have starved within the castle walls and unleashes them upon the survivors as a ghastly, spectral host. Before any starvation rolls are made, the attacker selects a single unit. The attacker makes starvation rolls for this unit as normal, but any rolls of a 6 provide wounds to create a new Spirit Host. This unit may be placed anywhere on the tabletop, even inside the castle.

Rezziqueak's Warp-Doom Magma-Cannon   2,000 points

Skaven only.

The Warp-Doom-Magma Cannon uses the same profile as Warp-Lightning Cannon but has 6 Wounds instead of 4. To destroy the cannon in the pre-battle phase the opposing player must roll four combined 6s, rather than just one. The Warp-Doom Magma-Cannon cannot fire in the pre-battle phase. The cannon may be fired in the Shooting phase. Roll the artillery dice and multiply that number by 5: this is how many inches in a straight line the cannon fires. Anything under that line must be treated as if it has been struck by the *Cracks Call* spell. If a misfire is rolled, roll a D6 and see below:

1-3 Meltdown – The cannon explodes with a radius of 3D6" from the base. Any models within this area must take a hit equal to the strength of an artillery dice roll. If you roll another misfire the radius grows a further 3D6". Repeat until the strength and area of the meltdown is determined.

4-6 Overload – Roll the scatter dice, this is the direction of the cannon's fire for this shot. Now roll the artillery dice again and resolve the shot as normal.

DEFENDER'S SIEGE EQUIPMENT

Tower Upgrade: Haunted Mansion
500 points

Forces of Destruction only.

This tower was cursed by a powerful Necromancer many centuries ago, and the restless spirits bound to its walls haunt it even to this day. Any unit occupying this tower causes Fear. In addition, any enemy unit in base contact with the tower suffers D6 Strength 1 hits that ignore armour saves before combat begins, but these attacks still apply towards combat resolution. Note that only one Tower Upgrade may be applied to each tower section.

Witches Cauldron
500 points

Any unit and/or character in the same section as the cauldron may drink from it at the start of any of its turns. Roll a D6. On a roll of 1 the unit suffers D6 S3 hits with no armour saves allowed. On a roll of 2 or more one randomly selected characteristic is increased by +1 until the start of the unit's next turn.

Flaming Ammunition
100 points per unit

A defending unit that has a missile weapon (including a war machine) can be equipped with flaming ammunition. Once per battle, instead of making a normal attack, the unit can attack a war machine (including siege towers or battering rams) that is in range. Roll 1D6 for the entire attack, no mater how many models are in the unit. On a roll of 5+ the target catches fire and is destroyed.

Cauldron of Boiling Oil
250 points per unit

May be used once per battle. Place the small round template within 3" of the Boiling Oil unit. Any model under the template suffers a Strength 4 hit with the Armour Piercing special rule.

Warded Tower
250 points

A tower section may be given arcane wards. Any unit occupying the tower has Magic Resistance 2.

Hell Gate
250 points

A hell gate has a Breath Weapon with a Strength of 4. The breath attack can be used in the Combat phase against units attacking the section with the gate.

Sally Forth!
250 points

The defender can attempt a sally to destroy one of the attacker's war machines (including things like siege towers or battering rams). For each sally forth that is purchased the defender can roll an additional two dice in the Defensive Artillery Fire pre-battle phase.

Tower Upgrade: Dwarf Brewhouse
500 points

Forces of Order only.

The smell of a good ale is often all that is needed to inspire a warrior's flagging spirits. The master of the keep knows this well, and has supplied this tower with several barrels of heady Dwarf ale. Any unit occupying this tower may drink the heedy brew in the Magic phase, restoring D3 Wounds as per the *Regrowth* spell. However, if a 3 is rolled on the D3, the unit is subject to Stupidity for the rest of the game. Note that only one Tower Upgrade may be applied to each tower section.

Tower Upgrade: Wizard's Tower
500 points

A Wizard has a repository of magical lore in this tower. Any Wizard who is in the tower at the start of the Magic phase is treated as knowing all the spells from his chosen Lore(s) of Magic. Note that only one Tower Upgrade may be applied to each tower section.

Tower Upgrade: Tower of Blood
500 points

Forces of Destruction only.
Whether through dark artifice, fell sorcery or blood sacrifice, this tower oozes pulsing gore, inspiring those within to ever greater heights of violence and slaughter. Any unit occupying this tower benefits from both the Hatred and Frenzy special rules. Note that only one Tower Upgrade may be applied to each tower section.

Tower Upgrade: Sigmarite Shrine
500 points

Forces of Order only.
A modest, but highly revered shrine to Sigmar is housed within this tower's walls, and is believed to house a relic that once belonged to the first and greatest Emperor. Any enemy models struck by the unit occupying this tower must re-roll successful ward saves. This applies to both shooting and close combat attacks. Note that only one Tower Upgrade may be applied to each tower section.

ARMY ROSTER SHEET

Hero of Legend:

Name/Type	M	Ws	Bs	S	T	W	I	A	Ld	Sv	Type	Equipment & Special Rules	Pts
Character													
Mount													

Notes, Famous Deeds & Mighty Victories:

Regiment of Renown: | **Composition:**

Name/Type	M	Ws	Bs	S	T	W	I	A	Ld	Sv	Type	Equipment & Special Rules	Pts
Trooper													
Leader													
Mount													

Notes & Famous Deeds:

Regiment of Renown: | **Composition:**

Name/Type	M	Ws	Bs	S	T	W	I	A	Ld	Sv	Type	Equipment & Special Rules	Pts
Trooper													
Leader													
Mount													

Notes & Famous Deeds:

Regiment of Renown: | **Composition:**

Name/Type	M	Ws	Bs	S	T	W	I	A	Ld	Sv	Type	Equipment & Special Rules	Pts
Trooper													
Leader													
Mount													

Notes & Famous Deeds:

© Games Workshop 2011. Permission granted to photocopy for personal use.